THE CLIMACTIC DECADES

OTHER BOOKS BY THEODORE BRAMELD

Japan: Culture, Education, and Change in Two Communities

Education as Power

The Use of Explosive Ideas in Education

Education for the Emerging Age

The Remaking of a Culture: Life and Education in Puerto Rico

Cultural Foundations of Education: An Interdisciplinary Exploration

Values in American Education (co-editor and co-author)

Patterns of Educational Philosophy: Vol. I, Philosophies of Education in Cultural Perspective; Vol. II, Toward a Reconstructed Philosophy of Education

Ends and Means in Education

Minority Problems in the Public Schools

Design for America

Workers' Education in the United States (editor and co-author)

A Philosophic Approach to Communism

The
Climactic Decades
Mandate to Education

THEODORE BRAMELD

PRAEGER PUBLISHERS
New York • Washington • London

To the memory of
my father,
Theodore Edward Brameld,
and
my grandfather
the Reverend George William Brameld

PRAEGER PUBLISHERS
111 Fourth Avenue, New York, N.Y. 10003, U.S.A.
5, Cromwell Place, London S.W.7, England

Published in the United States of America in 1970
by Praeger Publishers, Inc.

© 1970 by Praeger Publishers, Inc.

Library of Congress Catalog Card Number: 73–95663

Printed in the United States of America

Contents

Foreword

by Kenneth D. Benne

This book deserves a wide audience. First of all, I commend it to Theodore Brameld's colleagues. He has much to say as a gadfly to the most intimate of these—philosophers and philosophers of education. He urges them to reorient their efforts toward clarification and illumination of the dilemmas of contemporary men and women as they seek to live in, through, and beyond a crisis culture. His criticisms of their presently confining preoccupations come from a high, not a low, estimate of the potential contributions of philosophers to the planned evolution of mankind. So he speaks to them both in anger and in love.

He speaks also to all of his fellow educators, in schools and out, men and women who seek to stimulate and support learning in persons of various ages. He summons them to a responsibility at once both frightening and exciting. The responsibility is to help men toward "one overarching purpose—the purpose of a converging humanity engaged in ever-restless, ever-anxious search for its own ultimate meaning and its own deepest fulfillment."

Third, he has words of hope for the revolutionaries of our time, with whom he is, though not uncritically, identified—militant teachers, students, and blacks. The hope comes from his demonstration of the high potential of a reconstructed education to serve revolutionary objectives.

Fourth, he should be read by "Establishment" leaders who are still able to think rather than just to defend the *status quo*. For the hope of perpetuity for our major institutions, he seems to be saying, lies in their reconstruction through thoroughly reconstructed educational means and commitments.

What is the message Theodore Brameld brings to these various audiences? It is a vision of a future-centered education, alive and open to the threats and promises of a technological civilization which has lost its human bearings, and religiously committed to building processes of personal and cultural renewal into the fabric of an emerging world society.

As he struggles to give shape and coherence to his vision, Theodore Brameld tries to bring and hold in fruitful interrelationship inescapable aspects of human existence which are, on the surface, contradictory and which tend to fall apart in truncated and doctrinaire projects of life and education. It is his refusal to opt for one or the other of these unviable polarities that gives vitality to his philosophy of life and education.

I have identified five pairs of polarities which he struggles to bring and hold together in this book. First is the necessity of educating simultaneously for commitment and for objectivity. Second is the need to keep both social and personal values in mind in setting and evaluating the outcomes of education; hence, his overarching value of social-self-realization. Third is his continual attempt to do justice educationally to both the intellectual and the emotional requirements of fully human development and functioning.

Fourth, Brameld, while emphasizing the need for reorienting American schooling away from its customary stance of pseudo-neutrality toward moral, political, and religious issues, insists that value inquiries should be provided with an adequate factual and critical basis. Fifth, while insisting that educators focus committed effort toward articulating magnetic and compelling goals adequate to the task of building a world civilization, he counsels equally assiduous attention to inventing new and powerful designs and processes of teaching and learning.

While Theodore Brameld's main efforts in this book are devoted to projecting and clarifying goals for a future-centered education of mankind, his work does include a number of creative programmatic suggestions as to the means for their attainment. His chapters on experimental centers for the creation of world civilization and on anthropotherapy attest to this fact.

Again, I commend this work of a practical visionary to a very wide audience, inside and outside the profession of education.

Preface

The turmoil besetting education today is the perfect instance of a mixed blessing. Certainly it generates widespread befuddlement and, too often, violence. Yet, as in many other periods in the history of cultural affliction, it also provides magnificent opportunities for searching re-evaluation and re-creation.

Of several famous interpreters of this condition, one must mention Paul Goodman and Edgar Friedenberg. Is it not ironic, however, that neither of these critics—nor a number of others who have commanded wide audiences —can be regarded as a "professional" expert in education? To a remarkable extent, they write as social scientists or as sophisticated laymen, not as "educationists." The latter, indeed, are usually relegated to a very low place in the pecking order of virtually every academic or intellectual elite.

I am sorry to say that this position is about all that most of us "educationists" deserve. Nor is the target of criticism merely the busywork of teacher-training institutions or the pedestrian researches characteristic of most graduate programs in education. I am able to discover very little that deserves applause even in the one department within numerous colleges of education where we can most reasonably expect to discover provocative ideas and vision—that is, in the "foundations of education," which include, at least nominally, many "philosophers of education." At the very moment when we might suppose that educational philosophers, almost before anyone else, would be addressing themselves to the explosive issues and imperious demands pervading schools and colleges, much of their energy (granted a brilliant exception now and then) appears to be expended in rehashing John Dewey's pioneering contributions or in dissecting linguistic concepts after the manner of so many "pure" academic philosophers, or in other bloodless performances of extremely narrow scope.

Furthermore, even the most penetrating and widely read noneducationist writers about education concentrate far less often on its all-embracing, enduring problems and purposes than on relatively circumscribed obsolescences of time or place. By calling our attention to, say, the "vanishing adolescent" who is "growing up absurd," they do, to be sure, heighten our critical sensitivity. Some of their insights, moreover, cut very deep. Nevertheless, their usual emphases, enhanced though they are by an appropriate sense of urgency, obscure and divert attention from interpretations that may be less arresting but also should be much more inclusive, more fundamental, and hence more genuinely philosophic. It is just this kind of philosophic interpretation of the human predicament that is education's central mandate.

Even in blasé America, a few of our younger theorists are insisting more and more trenchantly that philosophy can become—just as it was at critical junctures in the past, extending all the way down from Plato and Confucius—a powerful influence on virtually every phase of the ubiquitous cultural institution that we call education. Equally, however, they are beginning to perceive that, if educational philosophy does once again achieve its rightful place in the life of thought and action, it will certainly not be because of the postures characteristic of most collegiate representatives of this discipline or because of the more conspicuous noneducationist interpreters of education.

Nor can this book, despite its plea for a radically energized conception of education, claim to do anything more than suggest preliminary corrections of the deficiencies to which I have alluded. Although for over three decades I have maintained fairly persistent hopes in behalf of exactly that kind of conception, I am the first to agree that the philosophic view of education with which I am associated, sometimes termed "reconstructionism," remains one of continuous groping and stubborn probing. As its critics have generously demonstrated, a good deal of conceptual refinement and experimental application is still to be undertaken, especially with the resources of philosophy and anthropology—the two fields through which I have sought most frequently to elucidate reconstructionism as both educational theory and educational behavior. Even so, I firmly maintain that this position, were it to receive sustained attention from citizens and scholars alike, could contribute substantially and powerfully to the clarifications and implementations of education now so desperately needed.

This book is submitted, accordingly, not in the spirit of resolution but, rather, in the spirit of invitation. Although it builds upon a number of earlier, more elaborate ventures directed at partially comparable interpretations, and although these ventures, too, are indebted to fundamental contributions by historical thinkers, social scientists, and others, the present work does take several additional steps. It discusses some of the same inflammable controversies that fascinate especially noneducationist interpreters. But it also seeks to bring philosophic ideas to bear directly upon concrete applications.

If any reader should wish at the outset to consider the framework of educational philosophy encompassed by the reconstructionist point of view, he may turn to the condensed statement provided in the Appendix.

Springfield, Massachusetts
February, 1970

THE CLIMACTIC DECADES

1. Introduction: Agenda for an Ecumenical Congress in Education

Let me resort to journalistic style by citing several fairly characteristic news items.

—The national organization of independent schools announces that for the first time in American educational history there will be a well-financed, nationwide attempt to break through the iron curtain of sex education.

—*The New York Times* runs a front-page story about a pilot public school soon to open in the slums of Brooklyn. Its faculty, with a citizen group, plans to reorganize the program from top to bottom, to make it relevant to both the children and the community.

—An educational journal features an article by a former president of the National Education Association to the effect that we must think of unionism *versus* professionalism in education.

3

—The General Electric Company and *Time* Magazine announce their decision to join forces to reorganize the technology of teaching—a multimillion-dollar enterprise. Meanwhile, *The Saturday Review* publishes an editorial on this matter: it is very well for *Time* and General Electric to combine their overwhelming financial power in behalf of automated educational learning and teaching, but what will this mean in terms of significant educational purposes?

—An entirely new high-school curriculum is to be constructed, backed by a large grant, in terms of anticipated cultural, economic, social, and technological patterns of living as we approach the twenty-first century.

—College students by the score are tear-gassed, arrested, expelled, shot at, and praised in a news summary of one week's events.

What do these items mean if we consider them together? Surely at the minimum they mean that excitement is pervading education—an unprecedented mood of excitement. No one, of course, could fail to perceive this. Yet how are most of us able to comprehend fully the familiar contention that, in the past twenty-five to thirty-five years, more new knowledge has been discovered than in the preceding five thousand years of human history? No wonder, then, that if this is a time of excitement it is also a time of bewilderment, of groping, and, above all (to go back again to the NEA item), of "versuses."

But amid the welter of conflicts and confusions, is it not also true that an eager searching for unity can be discerned? For example, how many of us, even now, have begun to grasp the import of the great ecumenical congresses in Rome? It took profuse and prolonged sessions for these congresses to complete their agendas, and then, of course, they did not really finish. Inspired by the late Pope John, a new urgency toward convergence among at least the major religions of the Western world was recognized in a way that disturbed traditions, customs, and attitudes by the hundreds. In fact, when we look at education and compare it with religion, do we not often find much more resilience and leadership in religion these days than in education? Take the civil-rights movement and the martyred Reverend Martin Luther King, Jr. A religious leader, he contributed enormously to changing the mood of a great nation.

Religion and education, it could be argued, are the two primary and universal institutions of mankind. Granting that religion leads education at present—certainly in terms of its quest for a new interreligious, intercultural approach to the common denominators of human life—what education very much needs today is a fresh audacity of its own. Therefore, I present for critical consideration an agenda for an *ecumenical congress in education*. This attempt will certainly raise more questions than provide answers. Even so, we cannot develop objectives for American education— much less for education concerned with the world as a whole—until we confront the necessity to resolve the acute disagreements that now pervade education on every level and in almost every culture.

Herewith, then, a 25-point agenda—or perhaps I should say 25 areas of uncertainty. Each of these areas suffers from stereotyping, rigidifying, closed-mindedness. In America, and in other countries as well, too many teachers and school administrators, too many college presidents and students, remain more inflexible than open-minded and resilient toward most or all of the issues that we shall now consider.

Because each of the 25 items invites an entire volume, not to mention the fact that still further items have had to be excluded entirely, I am compelled to be both sketchy and selective. But let us simplify the matter even further by grouping the items under three major headings:

CONTROL

1. "Unionism" *versus* "professionalism."
2. "Vertical" *versus* "horizontal" educational control.
3. Local or state *versus* federal control.
4. Segregation *versus* integration.
5. Private *versus* public financial support.
6. Parochial *versus* public education.

LEARNING-TEACHING

7. The "two cultures": scientific *versus* humanistic.
8. Specialization *versus* generalization.
9. Vocational *versus* comprehensive education.
10. Subject-matter curriculum *versus* problem-centered core curriculum.
11. Teaching machines *versus* functional teaching.
12. "Self" *versus* "society," or, in older terms, "child-centered" *versus* "social-centered" learning.
13. School *versus* community.
14. School *versus* home.
15. Noncontroversial studies *versus* controversial issues.
16. High school *versus* college.
17. Homogeneous *versus* heterogeneous learning and grouping.
18. Teacher *versus* student.
19. Research *versus* teaching.
20. Schools of education *versus* schools of liberal arts.
21. Education for nationalism *versus* education for internationalism.

EDUCATIONAL THEORY

22. Progressivism *versus* conventionalism.
23. Means *versus* ends.
24. Philosophy of education as linguistic analysis *versus* philosophy of education as world view.
25. Realism *versus* idealism.

Surely, all these items raise complex issues. This is why the proposed ecumenical congress in education must not become another "White House conference," another weekend gathering, but must be a congress that continues (as in Rome) for a year, two years, even three years. If the United States can afford to send men to the moon, it can afford to organize and support (with the help of other nations, of course, and of UNESCO, too) an ecumenical congress with sufficient time, patience, and energy to work through these conflicts.

For the fact is that each one of the issues stated in our agenda is ultimately *illegitimate*. Each one, that is, is capable of being reconciled on a higher level of synthesis, in which the strength of each "versus" is incorporated into a distinctive conception of education for our time—the waning third of our century that, we hear so often, may be the last century ever to be recorded by any earthly historian.

Now let us come back to our agenda and select certain items to exemplify this contention.

Take, first, the cluster of issues listed under "control." Item 1 refers, of course, to the National Education Association *versus* the American Federation of Teachers. Let us imagine a conference of representative educators assembled from around the country. Are we not likely to find a majority who are vehemently opposed to teacher unionism and perhaps a few who are just as vehemently opposed to the "company unionism" of the NEA (as it would be termed by any good union member)? The question: Is this kind of duality still defensible?

For several decades, the AFT has been maintaining that the teacher as employee has a perfect right to view himself as associated with the working people of America. One of the union's contentions, therefore, is that the teacher cannot hope to raise his economic status (and, through this,

his professional status) unless he engages in collective bargaining. Now, although "collective bargaining" is a term that labor has itself made famous, the NEA has adopted another term for virtually the same process—"professional negotiation." Is it not curious that the NEA regards "collective bargaining" as somehow beneath the dignity of the teacher, but that "professional negotiation" must not be so regarded?

These terms illustrate how easily we in education become entangled in semantic and emotional rather than meaningful issues. If we already agree that the teacher has economic rights, along with professional rights, that can be protected only by strong, united, autonomous organization, then surely there are grounds for rapprochement between the two organizations. Thus far, however, the AFT has too often been constricted by disputes revolving around economic conditions rather than wider educational concerns; the NEA, on the other hand, often pretends to be a representative organization of teachers, but its power structure has centered heavily in administrative echelons.

Granted that neither characterization is quite accurate today, the time has come for the two organizations to build a common front of unity based on the principle that teachers should control their own profession. They are the professional people of education just as doctors are of medicine (though I hesitate to draw an analogy between educational organizations and the American Medical Association). Much as we may disagree with the AMA on economics and politics, we must concede that doctors do run their own profession. Educators do not run theirs. They can never expect to achieve the status and influence that they ought to achieve until they do run theirs. Many NEA leaders would agree with this objective, I think; certainly all AFT leaders would agree with it. Therefore, a searching re-examination of our own fixed opinions on this matter is long overdue.

Consider the second issue: vertical *versus* horizontal control of education. The fact is—is it not?—that most of the schools and colleges of America, no less than those of most other countries, are still organized as line-staff structures. Authority funnels downward from the top administration through various subsidiary levels, until finally it reaches the teacher, the student, and maybe even the parent.

It is only too clear that this very structure is causing all kinds of disturbances and resistances today, especially in the colleges. Surely few can have forgotten the first Berkeley struggle of 1964, which was induced largely by the fact that many students at the University of California wanted a stronger voice in the control of an institution established in the first place presumably for their benefit. A remarkable report on Berkeley has since been prepared by a group of professors; it recommends many changes in regulations, courses of study, and participative procedures. And what or who chiefly brought about the writing of that report? Was it the president, the board of regents, the faculty? It was none of those groups; it was the students.

But California must not be singled out for too much attention. At Columbia, Wisconsin, Harvard, and dozens of smaller institutions throughout the country, including even high schools, ferment and discontent have been rife. As just one instance, student officers of one of our top-level high schools have issued a public statement to the effect that they consider the program of their institution to be largely obsolete.

Still, even this kind of incident is not really so extraordinary when we realize how little the structure of control has budged from its hierarchic, paternalistic moorings. Why, after all, do we seem to distrust students so much in cooperative decision-making? Oh, yes, "student government" is common enough. But one wonders whether most student governments are not also "company unions"—largely, if surreptitiously, controlled by teachers and administrators. Not that some structure of authority and control is not essential; schools do require leaders and directors. But does not this claim, too, beg the question? What has not been determined is how "vertical" authority can be more effectively integrated with "horizontal" involvement by teachers, students, and parents.

Our third issue, local *versus* federal control, has become increasingly exacerbated as unprecedented sums of federal money are made available for education. Here again, we are confused by semantics. Just as "professional negotiation" proves to be a smokescreen term, so the contention that federal aid is all right but control is not turns out to be false. We cannot have federal money allocated to communities and schools unless certain controls accompany that money. The proper question, which the NEA has often been facile in evading, is not control *versus* support at all but *what kinds* of control. Actually, amoral and immoral controls are intermingled with moral controls no less in education than in our own families and communities. The problem is whether or not democratic controls, which I identify with moral controls, can be developed on the federal level so that freedom for the majority is enhanced rather than decreased. Those who claim that increase of federal control necessarily means diminution of freedom argue on shaky premises. Would you say, for example, that the freedom of thousands and thousands of elder citizens has been diminished by the right to receive Medicare, simply because federal rules accompany that right? Well, the AMA may say so, but not some 80 per cent of the people, who, according to one public-opinion poll, support this new advance in public responsibility.

The fourth issue listed is segregation *versus* integration. Most of us have been concerned about this issue, but we often fail to consider that it is by no means limited to the black *versus* the white race. Other kinds of segregation are common in American schools, and other kinds of integration are, too. For example, one pattern of segregation is still prevalent in New England: separate private schools for girls and for boys up to and including college age. Even more segregation prevails when one thinks of socioeconomic classes in America. The Ivy League colleges and universities, for example, consist predominantly of students from the middle and upper classes of American society. If this is the case in these institutions, with their enormous endowments, part of which are earmarked for scholarships aimed precisely at reducing class segregation, surely it must be even truer of institutions that can afford to provide little or no comparable alleviation.

Class segregation is, in some ways, more insidious and widespread in American education than black-white segregation. We cannot deny, of course, that classes do exist in our society, any more than we can deny that there are a number of races and two sexes. A certain amount of clustering is therefore inevitable. But the problem that remains to be resolved in education is how we can find ways to recognize the existence of race, sex, and class differences, while at the same time providing maximum interaction among races, sexes, and social classes. The answers have not been well thought out.

The fifth conflict—private *versus* public support—is related to the earlier one of federal *versus* local control. Hence only a single point will be made here. Have we reached the point in our thinking where we are willing to recognize—to the degree, let us say, that the Soviet Union has done so—that education is a totally public responsibility? Most, if not all, students at the University of Moscow, for example, pay no tuition; indeed, they pay for neither board nor room. Whatever else one may think of the Soviet Union, the fact is that it is more consistent than the United

States in recognizing support of education as a national responsibility. Our own inconsistency is surely due, at least in substantial part, to deep-seated conflicts over the venerable issue of private initiative and public obligations. Just as these conflicts permeate economic and political life, so also they permeate education. No wonder that college students by the tens of thousands must take bank loans at shockingly high interest.

The issue of parochial *versus* public education must be bypassed here, although do we not again detect numerous straws in the wind? May not these two systems also be approaching new concerns of common interest?

The next major grouping, "learning-teaching," embraces both the content and the methodology of education.

Of the 15 selected issues in this category (no doubt others could be added), the first, symbolized by the term "two cultures," refers, of course, to the conflict between the sciences and technologies, on the one hand, and the humanities and liberal arts, on the other hand. That this, too, is a false dichotomy is suggested by Norman Cousins, among others. Education—indeed, culture itself—should be conceived, he argues, as a *partnership* of the sciences and the arts in a way that has not yet been conceived. Particularly since the passage, after sputnik, of the National Defense Education Act the sciences, along with mathematics, have received great emphasis in the schools, while the humanities and social sciences have come out no better than second best. The formulation of a policy assuring that no young person would receive any kind of baccalaureate degree until he had developed appreciation of the "third culture" of science and art in higher synthesis is another objective that ought to crystallize.

Overlapping this issue is that of specialization *versus* generalization. The term "general education" is itself one of the most vexing in the entire educational lexicon. Every educator seems to know what general education is, except that no educator agrees with any other about it. The challenge, therefore, of how to rethink this conception and relate it to the need for specialized education has not been faced squarely.

Somewhat similar observations may be made of item 9— vocational *versus* comprehensive high schools. This issue, too, is unresolved. Has there been any meeting of minds on the question of whether we should graduate young people from high schools with a broad education or, instead, with sufficient vocational training so that they can quickly market their skills? Or is not a kind of "third culture" or synthesis required here, too?

Issue 10 concerns the subject-matter *versus* core curriculum. In the past two decades or so, the drift has been very much in the direction of the former. Most curriculum experts seem to think that this issue no longer represents a live option. They seem to assume that it is passé to propose, for example, that the sciences and arts and social studies be integrated so that young people can graduate from high school and college possessed of some kind of a *Weltanschauung*, a view of the world as a whole.

But is it really true that we must educate students in more and more separate subjects and specialized areas— above all, in the sciences and allied areas? I do not think that John Dewey, in holding that integrated, problem-centered learning is the key to good general education, is obsolete either. The time has come for us to consider whether apologists for the educational Establishment have not obtained altogether too strong a grip on the public schools of America. If we repudiate the old dichotomies and begin to recognize that there is a place for both subject matter and unifying experiences, then such organizations as the conservative Council for Basic Education and the progressivist Association for Supervision and Curriculum Development both prove to be inadequate.

The related issue of teaching machines *versus* functional teaching is another that is scarcely resolved. Does the solution lie in simple, downright opposition to teaching machines? Certainly not. The proper question is whether we can keep them in an appropriately subordinate place— whether, amid the rapid trend toward automating the learning process, we can enable the child to grow and develop to his maximum powers and not merely to develop greater dexterities in the name of learning.

This leads to the next agenda item—self *versus* society— since here the teaching machine once more becomes relevant. American teacher education has suffered far too long from another dichotomy, this time within the behavioral sciences. Many educators seem to believe that learning is almost exclusively a psychological process, while others (fewer in number) believe that other behavioral sciences, such as sociology and anthropology, can provide a quite different approach. This dichotomy draws us straight to the self *versus* society issue, because, for a long time, many American educators have believed that the primary task of education is to develop the individual child. In our attempts to do so we have tended to overlook the fact that the child is a member of society—that the development of society is, indeed, no less important than the development of the child.

We can cite a bit of evidence for the fact that an imbalance exists. Virtually every teacher in training is required to take at least one course in educational psychology—often several. But scarcely 5 per cent of all teachers in training in the United States take a single course in anthropology. This weighting in favor of learning centering, say, in the individual's capacity to benefit by a teaching machine, to the neglect of both the development of culture and the individual's relations to culture, is no longer respectable. If *all* of the behavioral sciences were brought into the educational process to a much greater extent than they have been thus far, the imbalance could be corrected.

School *versus* community, issue 13, is once more involved with other issues. But the point to emphasize is that the school still remains, typically in this country and for that matter in most others, an isolated institution. Of course, we pay lip service to the community. Many of us even escort children to museums! But when it comes to enabling learners to enter continuously into the life of the community, itself regarded as a classroom, we are still a long way from accomplishment.

School *versus* home, item 14, is an issue that varies in acuteness among different parts of the country. Certainly in Massachusetts, where I live, it is of very real concern— for example, whether to hold that sex education is entirely the responsibility of the parents, or to maintain, rather, that the school must assume more and more prerogatives. If the latter, as the news item I have cited implies, education as a responsible institution must then cope directly and honestly with sensitive, often very disturbing questions of behavior.

The issue of home *versus* school leads directly to issue 15: noncontroversial *versus* controversial issues in the school. Yes, of course, all of us believe in studying controversial issues. But the fact of the matter is that we do not provide nearly so many opportunities in the public schools as we pretend to do. Sex education itself is an example. If there is any topic that is controversial today, it is how to decide what sexual behavior is right and what is wrong; yet we allow youngsters to graduate from high school and college and to reach their decisions with little or no informed guidance.

There are at least two other areas of controversy in which,

it seems to me, the schools are almost equally negligent. One is the area of politics; the other of religion. Indeed, the the three most sensitive areas in the curriculum are those centering on changing patterns of sexual morality, explosive political issues, such as communism *versus* democracy, and the question of whether or not religion is a fit subject for classroom consideration. As for the third of these issues, those who suppose that the Supreme Court has closed the door to the study of religion are, I think, completely wrong. On the contrary, the Court has opened the door to the study of religion, not as one or another doctrine or as a system of absolute dogmas, but as a very important area of culture that should be approached with the same careful, critical tools of inquiry demanded by any other crucial issue.

Issue 16, high-school *versus* college entrance require-ments, is also a serious one, which I shall discuss in Chapter 4 and elsewhere. As for issue 17, of homogeneous *versus* heterogeneous grouping, this problem has not been re-solved either. Some of us say: certainly we have to have homogeneous grouping in the schools. But others say, especially if they happen to be under the influence of dem-ocratic philosophies of education, that homogeneous group-ing is a euphemism for a kind of segregation—a kind that may produce prejudice and insecurity in children without their even being aware that it is happening. This matter is a complex one, and I do not pretend to offer a facile answer. I do suggest that if we were to re-examine it in terms of the strengths and weaknesses of both positions, we could de-velop a far more viable position than is now typical.

The issue of teacher *versus* student is also tempting to discuss at length. I can only suggest now that the schools of the world still seem to a great extent to be engaged in a contest between teachers and children, or between profes-sors on the rostum and students sitting meekly before the professors. The idea of a con*test*, exemplified in the traditional examination system, is a false notion of what the teacher-student relationship ought to be. Obviously this issue is related to others such as the subject-matter *versus* problem-centered curriculum.

Research *versus* teaching is a question that troubles many of us on the college level, but I must hasten to issue 20— the issue of schools of education *versus* schools of liberal arts. Certainly it is true that most professors of education are, to say the least, downgraded by their colleagues in the liberal arts. It is equally true that the chronic hostilities between the two faculties are severe in many institutions. This is an outrageous situation. Colleges of education do have something very important to contribute, and certainly colleges of liberal arts do also. The need for rapprochement could be met to a far greater extent if the faculties of the two schools were to talk frankly to each other. Each certainly has its weaknesses, but each also has its strengths.

To turn to the last large category—the theory of education—let us consider each of the four issues cited.

We have anticipated issue 22—that of the progressive *versus* the conventional approach to learning-teaching. This issue, too, is far from resolved. The new pilot school to be developed in the slums of Brooklyn is based, without doubt, on the progressivist philosophy much more than on what might be called the essentialist. Yet it is still very much an exception and will surely be opposed by many of the latter preference. At any rate, this issue penetrates very deeply into the meaning of human nature, of culture, and thus into the philosophy of life itself.

A comparable point can be made regarding issue 23: means *versus* ends. To a great extent, American education has become means-centered, just as American culture remains largely means-centered. We are marvelously dexterous at building teaching machines—and at selling them, too.

Part I
Education for the
Future as Reality

2. Imperatives for a
Future-centered Education

Education during these waning decades of
the twentieth century is confronted by one imperative before all others. This is to engage in a radical shift away from
both traditional investigations of the rich history of the
past and exclusive concentration upon contemporary experience. The shift that is now required is, above all, toward
the *future*. The character of this future, although profoundly influenced by both the past and the present, is of
distinctive and urgent importance for all dimensions of
education—including, perhaps centrally, the college and
university.

Such a theme is by no means novel. And yet the priorities that it now generates are, in crucial respects, novel
indeed—novel because the future that confronts us is
fraught both with threatening dangers and with revolutionary opportunities. One of our perplexities, therefore,

is double-edged: how, on the one hand, it may be possible to challenge the familiar complacency of vast numbers of teachers, students, and administrators toward such dangers and opportunities; yet how, on the other hand, to galvanize this challenge into imaginative, audacious innovations in the theory and practice of learning-teaching, curriculum, control, and every other feature of the educational enterprise.

Let us first reconsider the elusive meaning of time itself —a concept that has troubled philosophers for many centuries. In anticipation, it happens that I have been re-examining a book written by my own great philosopher-teacher, George Herbert Mead: *The Philosophy of the Present*, published in 1932 as the Carus Lectures.

Immediately one notices Mead's frequent use of a term that must have been more common among philosophers some forty years ago than it is now—the "specious present." By this term is meant, very simply, the brief period of time that extends both backward and forward beyond the instantaneous, fleeting moment—perhaps a fraction of a second —that, literally speaking, is the *only* present. Thus the specious present is specious in the sense that it is only apparently present. Its function is to encompass any given period of time as a kind of flowing wholeness by virtue of its continuity through both immediate memory of what has just occurred and imagination of what is about to occur.

In Mead's own approach to time, we may assume that the specious present also reflects an organismic rather than atomistic interpretation of reality—that is, a reality of relativistic space-time and of field or pattern rather than of discrete, separable elements. Certainly the specious present has no exact, measurable boundaries. It might be a "now" of only a moment or two, but it might also embrace a day or a much longer period, depending upon the vividness and pertinence of the experience.

In any case, the elasticity of this idea of time has been further clarified by twentieth-century philosophers of history. R. G. Collingwood, Herbert Muller, and others have persuaded many of us that even the past is by no means so "irrevocable" and so determined by causal chains of events as was widely accepted by earlier philosophies of, for example, classical realism, dialectical materialism, or objective idealism. Rather, "the uses of the past," in Muller's term, permit—indeed, require—continuous reinterpretations of history encompassed by ever-widening specious presents. In short, we have learned, perhaps more convincingly than ever before, that in this sense history, too, remakes itself.

But if we are thus enriched in our understanding of the past, at least equally may we be enriched in our understanding of the future. Contrary to Aristotelian and other classic views of the developing universe, including man's history, the future is no longer widely interpreted as governed by inviolable laws of predetermined destiny. Rather, by Mead and other philosophers of our age, it too is regarded as both malleable and creative.

Moreover, such an inclusive, dynamic view of time in general, and of history in particular, is by no means reducible to our own private, subjective notion of the specious presents we experience. In some instances such a notion may seem appropriate. But in others, the specious present may depend still more fundamentally upon the condition of a cultural period in which the flow of time is shared acutely by many participants of that period. Mead himself was too keenly aware of his own culture and too seminal an interpreter of the *social* processes of human life to have overlooked the cultural character of time. Does it not seem plausible, therefore, that he should have directed his attention more intensively to a "philosophy of the present" than to a philosophy of either the past or the future? Is it not indeed likely that he was reflecting, at least implicitly, the pervasive quality of his own transitory period of history? (He died in 1931 at the age of 68.)

For, in many complex ways, that period was one of short-range rather than long-range concentration upon political, social, or other pronounced characteristics of the milieu, especially the American milieu. Despite the Great Depression, despite even the convulsions of World War I fifteen years earlier, the prevailing mood was still one of optimism and smug self-confidence. Following the collapse of the League of Nations, America's pride in its own sovereign superiority continued to bloom. Technology was fast burgeoning. Progressive education, fortified not only theoretically but to some extent practically by Mead's close friend Dewey, was increasingly permeated by a comparable mood. No wonder that the specious present aptly symbolized a continuum of limited cultural attention and therefore of circumscribed duration.

Nevertheless, as I have already suggested, the specious present becomes a remarkably flexible way of interpreting time. Just as cultural patterns have fluctuated rapidly in subsequent decades, so, too, we are coming to question our former easy confidence in our capacity to live, plan, and act within such narrow ranges of time. Rather, the compulsions of our age—an age which has become awesomely, disturbingly different in the brief period since George Herbert Mead's time—now become the compulsions of our future.

We cannot, of course, document here the depth and breadth of this difference. We can only assert that many of the most perceptive observers of our age regard contemporary civilization as not only one of the most explosive, but potentially by far the most destructive, of all periods in the history of man. It has become commonplace to speak not of one but of *multiple* revolutions—revolutions in every major phase of human life, from politics and economics to science, art, religion, and morality.

But an age of revolution, as history abundantly reveals, generates abnormal concern about the future precisely because the consequences of revolution are so unpredictable. True, those who foment and join in revolutions are not themselves always clear as to just what it is they want to achieve; perhaps they are revolting *against* what they regard to be intolerable even more often than *for* an alternative. Yet, is it not also true that most of the greatest revolutionary leaders—Jefferson in America and Lenin in Russia, to recall but two—were articulate proponents of the directions and goals of the future that they hoped to achieve no less than they were opponents of the old institutions that they hoped to replace?

In either case, the specious present of each revolutionary period awakens the necessity of embracing a wider circumference of time than is characteristic of stabler, more confident periods. Equally, such a specious present incites both creative historical reinterpretations and, what is more to the point here, futuristic interpretations. Nor should these interpretations be regarded as simply intellectual. The specious present, although it always prevails more or less vaguely, acquires in revolutionary times a cultural as well as a personal vibrancy. Such a time is our own.

Surely it should no longer be necessary to emphasize that the needed new focus upon future expectations in no way disparages continued attention to the past and present. Nevertheless, three principal implications follow from this new focus. One is the frequently argued but still feebly demonstrated assertion that the study of history, as a scholarly discipline, itself acquires fresh relevancy in the experience of learning; thus we may anticipate that the pedestrian, sterile ways in which chronicles of the past are frequently taught to young citizens can become superseded by the indispensable role that history plays in elucidating the present and, even more, the future of man. A second implication is that the specious present at once acquires sharper tone as its boundaries are stretched to embrace the future that revolutionary events portend. The third and, in terms of our thesis, most momentous implication is the deliberate, systematic need to provide substantial places in the curriculum, and on every level of learning (adjusted, obviously, to the maturity of the learners), for concentrated study of the future. I turn next to illustrations of how this kind of study could and should contribute to the creation of still another revolution—in education itself.

One of the first tasks that awaits us involves meticulous, prolonged examination of what I shall call "scales of expectation." By this somewhat crude term I mean the development of a paradigm of the future ranging from, at one pole, a *maximum* of plausible expectations (that is, anticipated achievements) to occur during within, say, the next three decades, to, at the other pole, a *minimum* of assured expectations.

In human affairs, even maximum expectations are, of course, more contingent and therefore less certain than are the expectations of a specious present that encompasses nonhuman predictions—next year's eclipse, for example. Nevertheless, an impressive roster of experts is already aiming at one dramatic target: the year 2000. An entire issue of *Daedalus* was devoted to this objective. A corps of scholars assigned to the Harvard University Program on Science and Technology is now involved in a ten-year period of research into the expectations of coming decades. The Society for the Study of Futurology has been organized in Frankfurt, Germany. The World Future Society has been in operation for some time, with headquarters in Washington. Another well-organized venture, the World Order Models Project, is of impressive proportions. The Institute for the Future, which embraces both philosophers and social scientists, has already issued several publications, including the recent book *Inventing Education for the Future* by seventeen scholars. The Council for the Study of Mankind, consisting of authorities in several fields, has devoted nearly twenty years to exploring planetary human goals and designs. Meanwhile, such influential thinkers as Lewis Mumford in America and Lancelot Law Whyte in England have expended their talents for many years upon troubling questions about "the transformations of man." The work of all these and many other groups and leaders highlights both the precariousness of the future and the astounding opportunities for cultural renascence that *could* occur in less than half a century. All these insist, too, upon searching diagnosis and prognosis of the polarities of maximum and minimum expectations.

One graphic case of what we mean by expectation is the population explosion. Only half a decade or so ago, many demographers were predicting that world population at the start of the new millennium world be six billion people. Recently, however, several authoritative statements have been pointing to a total of seven billion, some 15 per cent higher than the earlier prediction. This expectation is, of course, a statistical probability based upon current rates.

Another example almost equally alarming is that of increasing pollution across the planet. The UNESCO magazine, *Courier*, has anticipated not only an epidemic of poisoned water, air, vegetation, and animal life but also a threat to life expectancies in the human species itself.

Technology, which is of course a primary ingredient of both the population explosion and the pollution menace, also abounds with expectations—many of them destructive but others constructive. Upheavals in urban life, for example, with the accompanying overcrowding and planlessness, are to some extent counterbalanced by a vast range of inventions that already surpass the most prodigious fantasies of science fiction. Consider the research studies of the Hudson Institute, headed by Herman Kahn, which alone has compiled hundreds of maximum or near-maximum expectations, some well on the way to realization. I select merely a few at random:

—three-dimensional photography and television
—human hibernation extending from months to years
—control of the sex of unborn children
—permanent inhabited undersea installations
—general adoption of cybernation and automation
—artificial moons for large-area lighting
—programmed dreams

At the opposite end of the scale from Kahn's maximum expectations are the minimum expectations, thus far, of world peace and accompanying international order. No sophisticated student of the future confidently predicts the early attainment of either of these goals. Yet, ironically enough, many venture strong *negative* expectations—namely, that *unless* peaceful order is established soon, the already available stockpiles of nuclear power, not to mention equally available weapons of bacterial and chemical warfare, can liquidate *one* problem of the future very quickly and effectively. This is, of course, man's own survival, the likelihood of which decreases in direct proportion to increases in the ever more fearful fuels of death.

I suggest, however, another and no less essential approach to our "scales of expectation." As I use the word "expectation," it actually includes at least two implications. Some events may approach total predictability (*e.g.*, the coming of night). But other expectations connote a high degree of hopeful anticipation, even aspiration (as when a mother is "expecting" a wanted child).

The two implications are not necessarily antithetical. For, with regard to such auguries of the future as we have been exemplifying, predictive expectations may in some decisive cases prove alterable by virtue of the strength of aspirational expectations themselves. Consider again the exploding of population, or the polluting of nature, or the compounding of armaments: any one of these three expectations, given current rates of probability, still depends upon *one crucial variable*—man's foresight and capacity to direct and shape the course of his own evolutionary future. He *can*, if he so chooses, plan in behalf of planetary abundance commensurate with controlled population. He *can* achieve an international order strong enough and democratic enough to eliminate war. He *can* dedicate himself to individual as well as cooperative life-affirming values.

To be sure, we must not confuse this matter by naively identifying "aspirational expectations" as one scale and "predictive expectations" as the other. Simultaneously, we must recognize that maximum and minimum polarities of expectation apply to both the aspirational and the predictive. Moreover, even in the case of maximum expectations, universal consensus seldom if ever prevails on either scale or at either polarity. Gigantic institutions still subvert the scientific planning of population: on the continent of South America alone, an annual growth of some 3 per cent is sanctioned by religious authoritarianism. Other institutions even more gigantic—namely, the corporate oligarchies of exploitation and profit—hasten the rate of pollution because (sanctimonious protestations notwithstanding), they care very little indeed about the wellbeing of human beings or of any other creatures of nature. Worst of all is the industrial-political-military complex that benefits by boom-

ing armament campaigns which never reach rational boundaries, simply because there are none.

And yet, as we know, evil expectations such as these are
repudiated by most people of most nations, or would be if
only they could be made aware of them and were able to
consider and develop workable alternative aspirations. Here,
I insist, the two scales of expectation—the aspirational and
the predictive—need not remain as dichotomous as some
of us, including some philosophers, like to believe they are.
Recall once more the population explosion: surely, if great
numbers of people understood the dangers of a Malthusian
planetary cataclysm, or if they were simply informed and
freely aided to practice family planning, would they not
join willingly in a worldwide program to bring the rate of
procreation down to manageable rates? The irony here is
monstrous: we already *know*, scientifically, politically, and
educationally, how to solve this problem, for we are already
demonstrating in some areas of the earth that it *is* solvable.

The same point applies equally well to the control of
pollution, to the elimination of many chronic diseases, and
to numerous other expectations that most people in the
world would gladly endorse. Above all, most people would
surely support scales of expectation that could lead to both
the abolition of war and the establishment of viable agencies of peace. How many millions are aware of the bitter,
dreadful effects of so useless and cruel an undertaking as
the Vietnam war? But how many millions are aware, too,
that peace does sometimes occur, after all, and with it the
security of work and play, of family solidarity and comrade-
ship, even of trustfulness?

This is not at all to say that any realistic confrontation
of the future can afford to underestimate the vast difficulties of attaining even minimum, not to mention maximum,
expectations. Nations have not yet begun to approach
agreement that world sovereignty alone can avoid the de-

structiveness and instability of national sovereignties. Nor
are political scientists able to tell us with confidence whether communism, or democracy, or fascist-tainted dictator-
ships, or racist nationalism, or some other powerful ideology
will thrust forward to a position of domination. Even on
the psychological level, minimum expectations as to the
development and character of personality remain largely
unsubstantiated: human nature, shaped by both cultural
and scientific conditions, seems almost as capable of undergoing metamorphoses for destructive and conflictive ends
as for harmonious and fruitful ends.

Yet, is not the very fact that such complex conjectures
of minimum expectations remain undeterminable exactly
the reason that they, no less certainly than those of maximum expectations, deserve serious consideration by educators? Indeed, the more problematic either minimum or
maximum expectations prove to be, whether on the predictive or the aspirational scale, the more compelling they
become. For where else than in education, after all, can
these expectations be successfully confronted while time
still remains?

As the preceding question implies, the case for protracted,
penetrating study of the future is by no means established.
To affirm that effective resolutions of human problems of
the kind I have selected are probable, or at least possible,
is to affirm that education plays a much more responsible
role than that of "study" alone. It becomes an active, aggressive partner in testing and effecting such resolutions—hence
it becomes also an agent in the extension of a wider, more
importunate specious present than has thus far been clearly
recognized.

This contention may now be supported with the aid of
a further intriguing concept—"self-fulfilling prophecy"—
adapted both from its original sociological formulation by

Robert Merton, and from the more recent insights of the philosopher E. A. Burtt. In the latter's succinct language, self-fulfilling prophecies are "predictions that may affect their own outcome."[1] Or, as I should prefer to say, they are future expectations that are more likely to occur because we are already convinced that they will. Such expectations therefore depend upon some prior image of their character. Subjectively, to take an instance, if a man becomes convinced that he is an inferior person—because, let us say, he is a black or a member of some other minority group—then he tends to translate this image into his own behavior: he fulfills his own prophecy. Objectively, a comparable result often occurs: much of the history of the South has been predicated upon the assumption by whites, and even by many blacks, that the Negro belongs to an inferior race; cultural policies and programs have been instituted to demonstrate the inevitable consequence of this belief. Often, too, the scientists of human prediction encourage self-fulfilling prophecies by inviting us to believe that, because a strong trend already prevails—for example, toward further and still more frightful wars—then we must acquiesce in that trend through tactics that increase their likelihood.

But self-fulfilling prophecies may produce entirely opposite effects. The transformation now occurring in the attitudes of millions of black citizens is another case in point. To cry repeatedly that "black is beautiful" creates a new image of blackness itself; thereby it also contributes to strategies of "black power" as a self-fulfilling prophecy of that very proud image.

Sometimes, however, the awareness even of an expectation on the scale of maximum predictability can serve to deflect future outcomes by substituting more radically aspirational ones. Thus the science of demography can contribute very importantly, if indirectly, in building programs of alteration rather than of acquiescence in the currently rapid trend toward overpopulation. In one dramatic instance, an entire nation has fulfilled its own prophecy that strictly regulated population growth is entirely practicable by means of concerted educational, political, and scientific planning. I refer, of course, to Japan.

Grasping and applying the meaning of self-fulfilling prophecy to education thus becomes a prime necessity. Polite manifestations of interest in the future will no longer do. The philosophy and science of "futurology" requires nothing less than intensive, sustained attention to and search for agreement upon both trends and goals which at once approximate our maximum aspirations and strengthen the powerful instrumentalities required to achieve them. In short, the specious present, viewed in this context, embraces *both* revolutionary, aspirational ends of the future and necessary, testable, scientific means to ensure that they are won.

I have already pointed to the target of such ends and means. They are so well summarized by Robert Heilbroner in *The Future as History* that they warrant a few of his own words. From his reading of the past and present, Heilbroner finds three "general historical tendencies . . . firmly in the saddle": the increasing "impact of science and technology on civilization, the end effect of our egalitarian political ideas, [and] the ultimate organization of collectivism." Heilbroner himself is convinced that, "short of the profoundest change in the character of our civilization, or an incalculable redirection of events, they bid fair to dominate the social environment of the future."[2] I might add that all three of these future directions also abound with such complex problems and tasks that they constitute, in themselves, a virtual enjoinder for the education required of today and tomorrow.

Let us examine some of the implications of such an enjoinder. I am able, of course, to choose only a few recommendations that seem appropriate within this framework.

First, experimental designs for undergraduate general education should feature interdisciplinary programs of study and action centering in the great problems endemic to our civilization. Building upon comments anticipated by Chapter 1, the suggested design should move much further, incorporating both historical and contemporary knowledge and also providing room for familiar skills and specializations. Even these conventional roles should be thoroughly imbued with and hence affected by the unifying theme of minimum as well as maximum expectations in the comprehensive meanings I have tried to indicate. Such a design must not be envisaged as in any way either superficial in its standards of scholarship or neglectful of any major academic discipline. Nevertheless, the design must inevitably lead, on the one hand, to the elimination of large segments of subject matters whenever they are retained for no better reasons than those of routine or conventionality; it must lead, on the other hand, to the inclusion of other large segments that are now ignored or treated cursorily. Such a design implies, finally, that very few of the impelling perplexities of contemporary man can be treated exclusively through separate courses or separate departments; therefore it requires the construction of venturesome bridges across multidisciplinary lines.

Equally important to innovated general education are built-in provisions for involvement in depth with learning experiences that test ideas in the laboratory of living cultures. One example already under way has proved its practicality in some universities and colleges: I refer to programs in urban renewal—not renewal in any truncated sense, but in terms of the entire gamut of economic, political, esthetic, religious, moral, and certainly educational rebuilding for the future of the "city of man."

A second educational recommendation is that of programs for professional careers. Although this could be illustrated almost as well in the case of medicine or other fields, I select one area only—professional education. What I have urged as a governing theme for general education applies here also; every teacher should therefore be prepared centrally and regardless of his specialization on any level, including certainly the college level, to come to grips with teachings and learnings that bear most directly upon the future of man. Likewise he should experience direct involvement in both nearby and foreign cultures, especially as these teachings and learnings pertain to issues and prospects of the future of man.

More than this, schools of education, at least as vigorously as other divisions of the university, should set the pace for self-fulfilling prophecies of the goals of democracy to which they already pay more or less explicit allegiance. I refer especially to the very great need for fully *experiencing*, not just verbalizing, the captivating educational ideal of "participatory democracy." Certainly, prospective teachers who are to set examples of democratic values and behavior for students and communities should participate continuously in planning every type of curriculum, in cooperative learning through the art of dialogue, and in authoritative, not merely advisory, policy-making. Most professional educators have as yet made only token gestures in these directions. Typical institutions for teachers are severely hampered in the accomplishment of their professed objectives by line-staff pyramids of control.

Even more alarming, these institutions contribute heavily to the perpetuation of public-school structures that are still more dubious than their own. One can hardly expect teachers in secondary education, for example, to engage in vigorous attack upon the middle-class encrustations still typical of college-preparatory requirements so long as these teachers themselves are rarely prepared otherwise. In short, only as thoroughly innovated policies express in practice the full meaning of participatory democracy in theory can schools of education themselves hope to provide models for a democratic future.

Two further recommendations may be germane. One extends a suggestion offered by Margaret Mead some time ago: the inclusion of "professors of the future" in university faculties. Her point was that if it is important to staff every university generously with "professors of the past," and perhaps even more generously with "professors of the present" (in engineering, say), then surely it seems indefensible not to give systematic, equally expert attention to the remaining dimension of time. I would go further than Dr. Mead in urging several appointees, each representing a distinct set of competencies, organized into "Departments of Futurology" comparable to other departments in both academic stature and budgetary support.

A final proposal, elaborated in Chapter 3, deserves preliminary attention here. For several years I have been urging that some university pioneer in establishing an "Experimental Center for the Creation of World Civilization." Such a Center would be related closely to such other programs as the Department of Futurology. But it would differ in its completely interdisciplinary staff of philosophers, scientists, religionists, artists, and other scholars; in its high-level graduate program; in its field projects, extending to various parts of the planet; and in its unceasing cooperation with colleagues from every available country of the world, including Communist countries. All participants would engage in critical dialogues and explorations intended to decrease intercultural as well as international tensions, while aiming simultaneously to increase agreement and strategies of creative action.

How could it possibly be that a chapter purporting to deal with so radical a proposal should have thus far avoided any explicit comment on one of the most climactic events of recent educational history? I refer, of course, to student unrest and student power.

Although this question was touched upon in the introductory chapter, it has been deliberately avoided here for two principal reasons. The first is that everyone else has been talking about these occurrences anyway. And certainly everyone associated with higher learning, as recent conventions of the American Association of University Professors demonstrate, has his own opinion on what has gone wrong and what must be done to set it right.

My second reason is, however, more fundamental. It is that while I, too, hold strong opinions on these very irksome questions, I believe that I can express them best within the governing theme. For, while I severely question whether any one causal factor is *sufficient* to account for the worldwide rebellion of youth, I maintain that at least one *necessary* condition has not thus far received the attention it requires.

The explanation of this necessary condition I share with the social psychologist Kenneth Keniston, who, in his pioneering studies of college students today, has demonstrated that great numbers of these young people have lost their bearings. Haunted by an immoral as well as illegal war, bewildered by technological depersonalization, disenchanted with the value-orientations of their parents, and resentful of the often meaningless requirements for college degrees, increasing proportions of the younger generation have become insecure emotionally and uprooted socially. The

consequence is that the bland success and easy affluence
that was likely to satisfy college graduates of even one or
two generations ago is no longer satisfying. As a further
consequence, some of the "uncommitted" have become so
totally alienated that they find no path to the future at all
except through gross repudiation of the Establishment.
Others, however, like the "young radicals" to whom Keniston pays close attention, have begun to explore new
purposes and to forge new identities through creative opportunities for social and political action.

But I fail to discover, even in Keniston's astute analysis,
satisfactory explanations of the underlying weaknesses inherent in the specious present of our own time—a specious
present too delimited and too constricted by the cultural
period out of which we are only now struggling. Therefore,
I fail to discover anywhere adequate attention, either by
Keniston or by other interpreters of the younger generation,
to the necessary condition that has been so lacking and yet
that must now be satisfied. I refer, of course, to those
graphic formulations of revolutionary issues and indispensable expectations demanded by the future toward which
we are now racing.

In negative terms, to be sure, Keniston expresses much
of what both of us would prefer to express in positive terms.
Speaking again of the younger generation, he writes:

> . . . many of the social and historical roots of . . . individual
> alienation lie in . . . modern technological society—the loss of a
> sense of historical relatedness, the loss of traditional community
> . . . and, perhaps most important, the loss of a compelling posi-
> tive vision of the individual and collective future.[3]

The more positive responsibility which education is now
required to accept comes to fruition not only in the "loss"
of these characteristics but in the rediscovery and redirection of self-fulfilling prophecies that could transcend them.

In short, as we begin to generate a "compelling positive vision" out of man's tremendous capacity for individual and collective creation, this vision and this prophecy become more and more attainable. They become more and more attainable because, to recall Burtt's meaning, *predictions affect their own outcome.*

Meanwhile, let us recall another prophecy that underscores this meaning. For the first time in the known history of our entire astronomical universe, human beings have walked upon the surface of the moon. They have done so, moreover, precisely because technological genius provided the step-by-step, flight-by-flight instrumentalities of fulfillment essential to and governed by that prophecy.

In comparable ways, a future-centered education, cogently expressed in the noble symbols of philosophy, religion, science, and art, while harnessed throughout to concerted, militant action, can—indeed, must—fulfill another, far more urgent prophecy. This is the prophecy of a converging, peace-maintaining, yet ever evolving and adventuring community of mankind.

3. Experimental Centers for the Creation of World Civilization

A few years ago, the man admired by most of his peers as the world's most distinguished living philosopher led a great march and demonstration through the streets of London in behalf of nuclear disarmament. That man, although then approaching ninety years of age, was convinced that unless nuclear disarmament is achieved in the near future, humanity is in utter jeopardy. His name, of course, is Bertrand Russell. And for this action, he was jailed.

At about the same time, a man almost equally acclaimed by his peers, this time as the greatest contemporary German philosopher, published a book in America entitled *The Future of Mankind*. One of its themes is that atomic energy has made the self-destruction of civilization for the first time a literal probability. The philosopher's name: Karl Jaspers.

In America, meanwhile, no philosopher of even modest stature has been warning us in audible tones of the mortal danger that threatens contemporary mankind. A few other public leaders, to be sure, may speak in this vein—occasionally with vigor. But even when they manage to command a polite audience, rarely do most Americans appear to be listening.

Why is this so? Why does America, seemingly alone among great nations, appear to be infected with such chronic indifference, such callous calm, when it hears the voices of Englishmen such as C. P. Snow who, speaking before the American Association for the Advancement of Science, warned his fellow-scientists of his fear that the third and final planetary war will occur well before the end of this century?

To offer searching answers to these questions would require complex interpretation of the curious state of our American culture in this final third of the twentieth century. I have neither competence nor space to attempt those answers here. But I do assert that to the degree that the indictment is justified at all, the higher learning in America must accept a solemn share of responsibility. Where else, after all, if not in our colleges and universities, should America be producing men of the intellectual and moral stature of a Russell or a Jaspers? Certainly in my own field, philosophy, in which the larger share of professional scholars look with imperious disdain upon almost any philosopher who dares to confront the great contemporary issues of human life and death, one rarely hears of such men.

Yet, within our colleges and universities, many able scholars are to be found who, given just a little encouragement, would eagerly place their finest abilities, their highest standards, and their strongest imaginations at the service of an opportunity to respond to one issue that, before all others, we are now compelled to resolve: *Can the higher learning in America, hand in hand with that of other nations, contribute in vigorous and concerted ways to the creation of a world civilization*—the first world civilization on earth, a world civilization without which *all* civilization may abruptly end?

My proposal is one way by which this most urgent of opportunities can and should be faced with minimum delay. In brief, it calls for a substantial number of both large universities and small colleges to establish a closely linked chain of what I shall call, for the time being, Experimental Centers for the Creation of World Civilization. The precise structure and operation of each Center would vary with given institutions, one perhaps consisting of only three or four professional participants, another staffed by fifty or more scholars. Graduate students would be able to obtain master's or doctor's degrees, but undergraduates would be affected chiefly by feedback into their learning experiences through research and action programs developed in the several Centers. Thus, one of the chief functions of the Centers would be to provide radii, not only inward toward the sponsoring institutions where they are located, but outward toward nonparticipating institutions in various parts of this country and abroad.

Several basic features, despite differences, should characterize all these Experimental Centers for the Creation of World Civilization. A crucial group of assumptions grounded in the philosophy of education, the behavioral sciences, and other disciplines is less explicit than implicit in all these features, which may be regarded as a kind of policy platform for experimental implementation.

Each Center should proceed from the conviction of its participants that the world is confronted with unparalleled crisis, centering in but by no means limited to the fact that the Atomic Age is now well under way. We cannot possibly turn back. Upheavals in politics, economics, and technology, with their profound effects upon ethics, religion, art, education, and science, are all enmeshed with the undeniable truth that man, for the first time in history, now possesses the means to destroy overnight the nerve centers of every nation on earth.

We cannot, however, expect all faculty members of any institution to agree on even this assumed conviction. Even if most do agree verbally, we cannot expect all of them to behave differently. Proponents of any Center will find it debilitating to argue the pros and cons of the views of philosophers like Russell or Jaspers. Such a debate could delay any organizational decision indefinitely. The intention, then, is to enlist for the staff of each Center only those members of a given faculty who are already prepared to accept and declare that this first assumption is justified.

Despite the urgency of our first assumption, higher education cannot be expected to respond with enthusiasm to a largely negative motivation. The threat of atomic warfare, however monstrous, will not produce the kind of intellectual and emotional audacity that is now required. Attention must therefore be focused upon the need for a commitment to world civilization as the first imperative of our present age—indeed, as the one alternative that can, through the power of its constructive vision, defeat the forces of destruction. Scholars who join an Experimental Center would therefore be only those who willingly express such commitment as a condition of affiliation.

In the affirmation of normative commitment, this proposal deliberately departs from the tradition of "objectivity" and "neutrality" that has so largely permeated American higher education. Careful students agree that this tradition is not, in actual experience, so tenable or workable as it often appears to be. Rather, the history of higher education in America as well as in other countries reveals a welter of cultural values that shape curricula, influence research, and constrict the scholar's academic freedom to pursue the truth as he sees fit. But the imperfection with which the standard of objectivity has functioned is not necessarily a reason for repudiating it. Nor does the proposal advocate its repudiation for the institution as a whole. The standard of objectivity, however difficult to define adequately or implement practically, remains an admirable one.

What this proposal does advocate is a recognized place in the college or university for a group of scholars who are not only permitted but encouraged to indicate cooperatively and publicly what many of them may now indicate individually and sometimes only privately. In other words, the higher learning, at least in our age of upheaval if not in less troubled times, has an obligation also to provide deliberately for scholars who express bold commitments— in the present case, commitment to world civilization, as against the commitment to mere state or national policies that most of us already profess.

This kind of commitment is not to be confused with dogmatism or doctrinairism. The many scholars and other citizens already committed to the goal of world civilization rarely claim that they know the answers to the vast array of questions that such commitment immediately generates. On the contrary, the social scientists, philosophers, physical scientists, and others who have been working for years in the Council for the Study of Mankind, for example, have discovered that even the word "mankind" is exceedingly difficult to define in any profound or comprehensive sense.

At the same time, most participants in the deliberations of the Council would probably agree that world civilization, at least by contrast with the fragmentations and conflicts of races and nations that have thus far typified human history, does begin to acquire a core of planetary meaning. Thus, with the aid of so young a science as anthropology, men are for the first time coming to understand, not as a speculative wish but as a scientific fact, that human beings everywhere possess certain intrinsically common qualities, such as the capacity to love, out of which they may create common aspirations and eventually, perhaps, common institutions.

The significance of this second feature can be conveyed in another way. Can we not contend that the commitment to world civilization for *our* time is similar in crucial respects to the commitment of Thomas Jefferson, Thomas Paine, and other founders of our nation for *their* time? When they were first seriously challenged to conceive the image of a United States of America, they, too, were beset with bewildering, novel questions. Yet they, too, were fervently drawn toward a goal that could join together the disparate groups of the New World into a functioning unity. It was only when enough of them could agree on this kind of powerful commitment that they were able to go forward to the herculean tasks of specification—tasks that they finally accomplished by establishing the then-revolutionary federal system that governs us today.

The goal of world civilization, granted that it is more complex and hazardous to achieve, is still more urgent than the goal of a United States two centuries ago. The higher learning, meanwhile, has expanded in stature and power far beyond anything that even Jefferson's fertile imagination might have conceived. Its potential role in accomplishing for mankind as a whole what a few courageous, farsighted pioneers accomplished for one continent thus emerges as both a solemn and an invigorating one.

To establish still further safeguards against the dangers of authoritarianism and indoctrination—dangers that admittedly lurk in the radical value of commitment to purposes quite as often as irresponsibility and hypocrisy lurk in the traditional value of objectivity—every Center should provide unrestricted opportunity for critical reactions by all members of the faculty not directly associated with the Center policy and program. Some of these members will doubtless prove to be opponents of the whole purpose of world civilization; let them then, with utmost candor and realism, analyze every element of that purpose as it may develop through the research and theoretical activities of the Center itself. Through an open, uncoerced dialectic of scholarly disputation, every aspect of the program should be subjected to a self-correcting, public process of dissent and consent alike. Only thus can errors be exposed, weaknesses corrected, and proposals sustained.

The Center personnel should also become interdisciplinary throughout. Proposals of world civilization cannot be fashioned by philosophers alone, or by political scientists, or by any other single group of specialists, however much they may be concerned with the Center's rationale. Actually, the more cross-departmental the better: artists as well as scientists, religionists as well as educators, psychologists as well as sociologists—all should be included whenever and wherever scholarly resources prove available. Also, when circumstances permit, scholars should be invited from other institutions, including foreign ones, both to augment the staff on a relatively permanent basis and to provide an exchange of visiting experts from other Experimental Centers. The rich experience of the Center for

Advanced Study in Behavioral Sciences at Stanford should be drawn upon—even though its own interdisciplinary structure is considerably narrower than the one proposed, and even though the Stanford Center is governed by no encompassing commitment through which its members channel their exceptionally diverse abilities.

A chief purpose of the proposed interdisciplinary policy is not only to assure a broad flow of investigations but, equally, to guard against the congealing of commitments into intellectual or emotional rigidities. The free play of criticism, the principle that no conclusion ever reached is irrevocable, the experimental approach to every venture —all are enhanced not only by the steady flow of communication between the Center proper and the wider academic milieu but also by the pluralistic character of each staff itself.

The title suggested, please recall, is "Experimental Center for the *Creation* of World Civilization." It is now important to elaborate another key feature—namely, that the Centers should be concerned with action as well as with study, with practice as well as with theory, with means as well as with ends. The emphasis intentionally placed upon the end or goal of world civilization is hereby counterbalanced by an equal emphasis upon the role of the higher learning in reducing conflict by direct participation in worldwide planning.

Once again, therefore, the idea of the Center departs from one of the conventional standards inherent in much of our education. Not, of course, that colleges and universities have taken no part hitherto in community programs concerned with social change. Of course they take part, in slowly increasing degree. On the whole, nevertheless, this kind of participation has tended to be hesitant, piecemeal, even stultified by the standard of alleged objectivity.

And yet, how many of us would deny that education on every level is already involved, whether it always professes so or not, in the perennial conflicts of the wider culture? One need only recall the nightmare of McCarthyism, the aftereffects of which may be dredged up from the quagmire of recent American history to poison academic freedom once again, or the zeal with which many institutions of higher learning have entered into defense contracts with the federal government, to demonstrate how pervasively, if at moments surreptitiously, political, moral, and other conflicts saturate curricula, research, administration—in fact, the whole educational fabric. These Experimental Centers would aim to cut through such ambivalences, pressures, and intimidations. They would insist, not only that education is itself the object of multiple conflicts, but that it is and should become both active agent and creative participant in virtually all of them.

Conflict, moreover, is far from an unmitigated evil. Actually, no institution responsibly concerned, as it should be, with the cutting-edges of our age can always seek to avoid the deliberate intensification of conflict if such intensification serves to advance long-range human values. On the contrary, the term "creation" means the kind of conflict resolution that is directed, on the one hand, by the overarching goal of and commitment to world civilization and, on the other hand, by the keenest methodologies and social strategies of action research that the sciences and arts are able to provide.

At this juncture it is equally imperative to clarify what the Centers certainly are *not*. Of course they are not *the* agents of planned cultural change toward world civilization or of any ready "blueprint" of a society to be sought. Political and economic institutions will doubtless continue to be major centers of power in behalf of any kind of basic change (unplanned and planned alike) for a long time to come.

Because, however, formal education is only one instrumentality that can be utilized in the struggle to advance toward world civilization, we need not infer that it therefore possesses no power whatever to intensify that struggle. Such an inference is defeatist to the extreme; it is precisely that kind of inference that has lately been heard in America among influential voices in the ranks of educational leadership—particularly voices seeking to persuade us that the whole experimentalist, progressivist conception of education as a creative social force is now out of date.

The proposed Centers, on the contrary, would insist upon the need for strengthening this conception. They would repudiate the neoconservative apologist for academic conventionality who helps to rationalize whatever indifference or complacency is chronic in education today. They would throw their full energies into cooperation with the United Nations Educational, Scientific and Cultural Organization (UNESCO) and other international agencies currently active in a vast range of action research. They would utilize to the full extent whatever skills and experience in community involvement are available in other divisions of the university or college. Above all, they would rechannel and integrate the often aimless and narrow effort now expended in this kind of involvement.

From the several preceding assumptions and guiding principles it follows that no two Centers could or should be exactly alike—hence every program to be developed by any particular Center should fit the resources, interests, limitations, and opportunities of each institution that decided to join in this frontier adventure.

Consider, as one example, the awesome problem, already discussed in Chapter 2, of the world's exploding population of the human species. In the context of commitment to world civilization, two highly complex questions immedi-

ately arise from this problem. The first concerns the maximum size and distribution of population that can be
maintained on our planet in, say, the year 2000 in a manner
commensurate with scientifically established standards of
living. The second question is: How can population expansion be regulated by family planning and other means so
that the goal of a rationally balanced population can be
guaranteed?

These two questions are by no means ignored by higher
education. This is all to the good. It must be conceded,
however, that they are usually treated sporadically if not
overcautiously by a variety of specialists with little or no
demonstration of the multidisciplinary approach that is
now required. Actually, the problem calls for a whole range
of experts in fields as diverse as demography, physiology,
political science, anthropology, and certainly philosophy.
An Experimental Center of the kind envisaged would cor-
relate individual efforts, focus relevant tasks, and reduce
waste motion. It would do these things, moreover, always
in the setting of the larger patterns of world conflict and
world order within which the problem rests and without
which it must fail of resolution.

Equally dramatic examples of potential agendas could
be drawn from the literary, musical, and graphic arts, from
medicine, from law, from religion—in fact, from every
field of learning that bears upon the Center's ends and
means. (And what field of learning does not bear upon it?)
We will, however, select only one additional example,
from education itself.

One of the frontier specializations now emerging in a
few of our larger institutions is comparative education—a
field that concerns itself with the vast range of educational
theory and practice throughout the world, at the same time
that it serves the admirable purpose, among others, of reducing the typical provincialisms of American classroom

teachers. Any Experimental Center for the Creation of World Civilization with resources in this field should adopt as one of its action programs a comprehensive approach to some of the tasks that educators should now be performing in, say, the world's underdeveloped areas—tasks in which colleges and universities could be governed by much clearer conception of their international responsibilities than they now reveal. A program of comparative education vitally related to such responsibilities is transformable from a polite and dreary description of national school systems to an aggressive partner in political-economic change. The comparative educator thereby becomes a full-fledged associate of the anthropologist, the demographer, the philosopher of education, and other disciplinarians. At the same time, he shares his experiences with colleagues and students in conventional teacher-training programs so as to enrich their own contributions.

I have tried to "zero in" on the central question facing our world today and to dramatize its urgency through a concrete, workable proposal. No one denies that much of what now goes on in higher education deserves commendation. At the same time, I do not suggest that Experimental Centers for the Creation of World Civilization should be considered as merely appendages to our already overcomplex and overburdened programs.

The focal question is one of priorities. To launch and operate a successful Center means that some other conventional courses or research activities will no longer exist, and that some members of the faculty will wish to substitute part or all of their older schedules for the pressing ones implied or stated in this design.

At the same time, it is scarcely realistic to expect that most of our largely eclectic and often opaque policies will yield to new imperatives in the immediate future. The wheels of higher learning grind slowly. What I propose is a practical way of facing the compulsion voiced by Bertrand Russell and other great thinkers. No serious financial obstacle impedes that practical way. *Almost any college or university with a nucleus of scholars of the kind I have described could, if it so wished, establish the beginnings of a lively Center within a single year.* Once the Centers are under way, the great foundations could offer generous support—so, too, might the federal government. The philosophy behind the Center reflects, indeed, the political philosophy of responsible world-mindedness that may now be dawning, not only in the United Nations, but in segments of our own political leadership.

The times in which we live are of such peril as to produce in many of us a kind of moral and social paralysis. Yet the rosters of faculties of our colleges and universities list deeply troubled men and women who perceive both the awesome dangers and promises confronting mankind at this juncture in its evolution. They await the opportunity to prove how ready and competent they are to translate that perception into a working synthesis of concerted action and defensible commitment. Experimental Centers for the Creation of World Civilization would provide them with such an opportunity while time still remains.

Part II
Insistent Tasks
Before Us

4. Illusions and Disillusions in Education

Insistent tasks before us, to which we now turn also very selectively, may be regarded as a bridge between what has been considered thus far and what we must now criticize and interpret more incisively. Therefore this chapter at once recapitulates and anticipates.

To recapitulate first, let us underscore forcibly the phenomenal unrest that permeates educational events. It signals a situation that has already succeeded in penetrating and, in some respects, even shattering the whole façade of beliefs, processes, and structures that hitherto seemed impervious, if not oblivious, to inadequacies in the vast institution of modern education.

The term "façade" is used deliberately because, to an extraordinary extent, education in America (in many other parts of the world as well) is now demonstrating itself to be an increasingly artificial, perhaps obsolete, enterprise—

artificial and obsolete in the sense that it distorts, conceals, and avoids many of the most fundamental perplexities and compulsions of our age. I should like accordingly to present a series of what may be termed great "illusions" and "disillusions" of contemporary education. By the former is meant, of course, the fallacies and shibboleths that remain only too apparent. The latter term, however, has more than a negative connotation: disillusionment is often the forerunner of reawakening and renewal. It is largely in this sense that I speak of "disillusion."

One cannot list all that might be included in such a series. With the aim of succinctness, I am compelled, as earlier, to oversimplify. Nevertheless, my examples should provide ample support for the contention that education today is being forged as a double-edged sword. With one edge, it proves a novel capability to cut through more and more of the façade; in this sense it plays the indispensable role of exposing its own obsolescences. With the other edge, it enables us to consider how this capability may be channeled toward more impelling alternatives—toward innovative beliefs, processes, structures, and especially toward newly emerging goals that are the fruits of its own disillusions.

Here, then, are ten of our illusions.

1. Education's primary task has always been and must always be to perpetuate the customs, attitudes, practices, and institutions that prevail from generation to generation. This still-dominant characteristic, although not always explicitly rationalized, is maintained not only by many educators but by remarkably large numbers of psychologists, sociologists, and anthropologists. Terms familiar in this context include "adjustment," "socialization," "enculturation," and "transmission."

2. It follows from #1 that the primary task of teaching

is to assure such perpetuation, thereby qualifying each successive generation for induction into and approval by adult society. This task is exemplified in modern America by the heavy emphasis placed upon preparatory curricula of the secondary school, and thus upon trainings that enable the young to gain admission to higher institutions of education, preferably those of such prestigious standing as virtually to assure the graduate's acceptance by the more affluent sections of that society.

3. Conversely, the primary task of learning is to respond to the task of teaching noted in point 2. Today, this capacity is being refined and accelerated by the new educational technology. With the proliferating automatized gadgetry, the learner can be increasingly "prepared" in streamlined factories of learning, hitherto known as schools.

4. Largely because of the assumptions embodied in paragraphs 1, 2, and 3, educational institutions have been effectively organized and controlled chiefly by means of hierarchical structures of authority centering in school boards and boards of trustees, and through these in their appointed representatives: college presidents, deans, superintendents of schools, principals, and lesser figures who determine policies and practices of learning and teaching. Students are expected to recognize and accept such authority, since this provides, after all, the legitimate basis on which they are admitted in the first place.

5. From #4 it follows that the proper role of the teaching profession is to perform duties established under the same hierarchical system. Such duties, being professional, cannot justify any behavior on the part of teachers, and still less so of college professors, that disturbs or departs in any notable way from the "professional" conduct already ordained by directors of this system.

6. From #4, also, it follows that the obligation of students is to perceive and respect established criteria of

knowledge and wisdom that those in authority have approved by virtue of academic appointments. After all, are not students in schools and colleges to learn from superiors assigned to teach them? This rhetorical question applies not only to the higher learning but, even more fully, to lower levels, where the immaturity and inexperience of the learners can be guided only by those who are qualified because they are mature and experienced.

7. From #6, we may infer that the responsibility of education, being primarily the continuous transmission of such cultural behavior as habits, attitudes, and wisdom, centers in those kinds of learning that are most widely accepted and most useful to society. These have differed at different times, but today they are characterized above all by the demands of industrial technology. Hence the curriculum, especially of primary schools, is weighted with the teaching of rules of social acceptability and such necessary skills as reading and writing, whereas that of the secondary school is weighted with such subject matters as mathematics and science to assure manpower for our burgeoning technology.

8. By the same token, characteristics of the curriculum that do not lend themselves directly to this supreme imperative tend, very properly, to be relegated to lower strata of importance. The musical and graphic arts in the primary and secondary schools are illustrative. Another example is the social studies: American history alone is considered an academic essential to cultural perpetuity, but other dimensions of cultural experience, because they are more liable to dispute and therefore to public criticism, are at best treated feebly, if at all. I refer, of course, to such dimensions as major political strife, class conflicts, religious issues, civilizations of the East or Africa, and dilemmas of international polity *versus* national sovereignty. Sometimes, to be sure, these issues are treated with care. But by and large,

they are not; and it is only another illusion to pretend that they are.

9. Education, like virtue, is a wonderful achievement, and almost everybody believes in it. But this is not to say that everybody believes the nation should provide financial support for this institution anything like the support provided for certain other institutions—above all, the military. Teachers and students should be grateful that the amount and proportion spent on education is currently by far the highest in our history. Americans also should feel gratitude that no federal authority supervises education. Just as most money is provided by local or state taxation, so too does educational authority remain, quite admirably, decentralized.

10. The same tradition is, of course, extended to the control of education on an international scale. Despite the magnificent efforts of UNESCO, we must remember that it is not and should not become an international educational authority. It is, rather, a vehicle for nations who may or may not wish to cooperate with it. Nationalism should remain the ultimate authority for education, just as it does for politics in the United Nations as a whole.

An extraordinary fact of today is, I believe, that not a single one of these ten attitudes, policies, or practices can withstand searching scrutiny. Some are perhaps less glaringly suspect than others, but all are beginning to waver. Others are threatened even now with virtual disintegration.

The reader will have observed, of course, that none of these illusions can be characterized as *totally* illusory. Let us then generously term them "half-illusions." But, like half-truths, half-illusions are treacherous. We have learned only too painfully from current political rhetoric that half-truths often prove to be more insidious than total falsehoods. It is these as much as total illusions that now compel us to view our selected series as, more exactly, disillusions.

1. The underlying and usually unstated belief that education is an instrument of social and cultural transmission is a case in point. Of course, education does provide indispensable cultural continuity. (This function is just as indispensable to so-called nonliterate cultures that have no formal educational systems at all.)

The distortion derives from steadily growing evidence that the learning-teaching process, inclusively defined, is rarely if ever reducible to mere transmission. Anthropological research (not always sufficiently noted, to be sure, by anthropologists themselves) demonstrates that all cultures undergo degrees of modification by virtue of the obvious fact that they are never static. More or less constantly, therefore, their members confront degrees of novelty, if only because the evolutionary process is itself always novel —a generalization demonstrated sometimes dramatically but oftener modestly in struggles to combat and control inanimate and animate environments. Anyone, for example, who has observed perhaps the most primitive culture on earth today, the Australian aborigines, is struck by the fantastic ingenuity with which its members search out and discover food, invent their own tools, and in many ways demonstrate abilities and skills suited to their arduous needs. How much more truly do complex and sophisticated cultures prove their own genius for originality, discovery, and inventiveness!

The point I wish to make penetrates still more deeply into the whole psychology of learning and teaching. It takes issue with the behaviorist assumptions that have recently obsessed so many psychological practitioners under the influence of B. F. Skinner and his followers. Surely, however, to belabor further the creative capabilities latent if not always overt in human experience is redundant. One has only to recall the amazing achievements that abound in the arts—in painting, the dance, sculpture, music, architecture, and others—through millennia of history and across all continents.

A great deal more could be said about our first illusion. Yet even these sparse remarks would be wholly superfluous were we not so often still muddled by the metacultural assumption that education is predominantly a "reinforcing" or "socializing" process.

2. The view to be repudiated here is that education (especially for the increasing middle classes of America, France, Japan, and other countries) must be designed primarily to assure the young, and even more their parents, that they should go to college, and that in order to do so they must meet the admissions standards established *by* the colleges.

Lively criticism has been generated against this complacent view. Not only are some of us beginning to question why the typical high-school curriculum should so often be tailor-made for the conventional college-bound student, but more seriously we question whether the curriculum is defensible even for such a student. To a shocking extent, both the high-school and the college curricula of today are the same in over-all structure as their counterpart of fifty or more years ago—an "egg-crate" of courses with little if any significant relation to one another or to the central streams of life around them. All, or mostly all, are still bound by the all-too-familiar rubrics of English, mathematics, science, social studies, and foreign languages, plus a smattering of peripheral subjects.

3. Until our second illusion is dissipated, the illusion that worthwhile learning can be successfully automated is unlikely to be challenged either. To put the point differently, as long as ambitious, competitive, grade-seeking motivations remain paramount, school and college hierarchies will respond eagerly to the high-pressure promotion campaigns of huge corporations. But the focal question is whether the

efficient stimulus-response kind of learning induced by this technology can actually produce "educated" people. Disillusionment lies in the greater likelihood that, given a free rein, it will produce excellently conditioned human beings but neither autonomous nor creative ones. *Brave New World* and *1984* are ominous but only too plausible alternatives.

4. The possibility of radical challenge to automation and computerization in education is remote, as long as our fourth illusion carries its own heavy burden of influence— namely, that the best organization of education is to be found in models of business, with directors and managers properly in command, and with lesser personnel of education largely subject to their orders. The line-staff structure of education is thus by far the most prevalent one.

It is also a major source of current student and faculty revolt. Behind this revolt, I submit, is an awakening if still semiconscious realization that the analogy with business models is blatantly false—that education should be conceived, rather, as an institution designed, not to reinforce efficiency or comparable virtues of the prevailing power structure, but to encourage critical-mindedness, distinctiveness, "dissentual knowledge," and participation by both students and faculty in every segment of educational life and on every level.

5. I have mentioned faculties here, and thus we return to the illusion of conventional teacher and professorial subservience to educational control. It would be difficult to find better samples of exposure to this illusion than a widely quoted statement by Mrs. Ruth Trigg, former president of the Classroom Teachers Association, a division of the NEA.

I maintain that a teacher who finds himself in a situation where conditions are such that good education is an impossibility, having exhausted every other means of improving those conditions with no success, should walk out. I further maintain that this teacher shows more dedication to his profession than does the teacher who stays on the job, perpetuating mediocrity. Perhaps the child's education will be interrupted for a week or a month, but what is one week or one month when measured against years of education, all less than adequate? If the teacher's militancy leads to improved conditions of learning, the child's opportunities are enhanced for a lifetime.[1]

Here, surely, is a remarkable repudiation of teacher mores. Yet it is only a more general statement of another even more pointed repudiation by David Selden, an official spokesman for the labor-affiliated American Federation of Teachers:

I think the best thing that can happen to the country is a nation-wide teachers' strike to bring about the vast improvement in schools that we need.[2]

If we recall events occurring in several cities in the light of what Mrs. Trigg and Mr. Selden have said, we must agree that illusion 5 may be on the verge of collapse. And if we underscore such a likelihood with the record of teachers' organizations in several other countries, we must perceive this phenomenon even more clearly. In Japan, for example, Nikkyoso, the national Teachers' Union, is not only the largest union in the entire country but one of the most militant, most politically minded opponents of the economic, social, and educational Establishment.

6. Closely related to the intensifying militancy of teacher power is, of course, that of students. Here again I can pinpoint the fallacy at issue by a quotation, this time from Professor Alain Touraine, of the University of Paris:

The student revolt is not merely a crisis of the adaptation of the universities to the modern society, nor is it only a revolt of youth against tradition. Rather, it signals the birth of new conflicts, the first act in the drama of putting the new, computerized industrial state on trial. But it is within the universities that its future lies, because it is there that learning takes place. The student movement is no longer the avant-garde of a peasant or worker movement, but the avant-garde of itself.[3]

What this means, I think, is that increasing minorities of students from Rome, Madrid, and Paris to Rio de Janeiro, Mexico City, and Tokyo are also defying the creaky apparatus, not only of learning-teaching, but of time-exhausted curricula.

The student upheaval invites a further point of far-reaching relevance. Profound, if also subtle and intricate, connections are traceable between student unrest and black unrest; witness the Cornell University struggles or, before that, the lunch-counter student sit-ins. But whether the alignment is tenuous or not, it is rooted in the malaise hinted at by Professor Touraine—a malaise typified by guilt, frustration, hatred, and (in the existentialist sense) meaninglessness.

This is not to say that the student and the black share *identical* travails. But they do often share *common* ones. The average black is the victim of white racism, as the Commission on Civil Disorders so impressively demonstrated. The average student is the victim of outmoded policies and programs which may just as ubiquitously, if often more covertly, generate negativism and skepticism toward education and its supporting triple structure of industrial, political, and military power. The students' and, to some extent, teachers' uprisings that have now become chronic herald a deep-seated want of self- and social fulfillment, just as the blacks' uprisings herald theirs.

The comparison may be carried further. Just as militant organizations such as the Students for a Democratic Society are inclined to reject the more classic sociopolitical theories of radical change, and along with them the dominance of the entrenched generation, so the black-power movement has rejected a good deal of the older liberal doctrines characterized by integration and equality of opportunity.

Once upon a time I, too, was much persuaded by these doctrines. As a staff member of both the Bureau for Intercultural Education and later the Center for Human Relations Studies (New York University), I tried to the best of my ability to contribute to such well-meaning integrative ventures. But today I am convinced that they have largely failed. Instead, I am inclined to sympathize far more strongly with such Negro leaders as I have come to know in the Roxbury ghetto of Boston—all of whom, from the most militant to the more moderate, regard black power as the clarion call of their programs. Moreover, after having read the deeply moving and enlightening *Autobiography of Malcolm X*, I hope that I am somewhat better prepared to identify with the mood of both blacks and students than I could have been earlier.

At the same time, let me seriously question whether the frequently defiant and disillusioning posture of student activism is any more mature or decisive an answer to student problems than black nationalism is to the problems of our Negro citizens. Both movements are manifestations of anguish, of strength, of courage, of self-respect, of group-identity. But both need to be superseded by a more clearly affirmative and powerful set of democratic strategies and goals. To recall the classic Hegelian concept, student power and black power are both in a stage of "antithesis" against the older "thesis" of traditional patterns. But both should strive to reach much further than this, just as Malcolm X had himself begun to strive further toward "synthesis" during the last months of his young and tragic life.

7 and 8. Both of these confront what I call "the disillusioned curriculum," with its overemphasis on the technological and its underemphasis on the esthetic, moral, social,

and humanistic. The correction of this situation lies in a thorough rebuilding of prevailing curricula of the public schools and colleges—a rebuilding already inherent in sweeping demands for maximum satisfaction of human needs and wants, and of great aspirations that hitherto have been recognized or gratified only in small measure.

Here again difficult questions confront us, for on paper there are almost as many curricula as there are curriculum planners. Yet the crucial question remains clear enough: whether learning and teaching, both as process and in substantive quality, can cope directly, constantly, and penetratingly with the central character of human life. Plenty of evidence points to the answer; indeed, some schools, all the way from Summerhill in England to Tamagawa Gakuen in Japan, are already proving that this kind of transformative adventure is both practicable and vastly exciting.

Of course, the curriculum envisaged here, and developed somewhat further in Chapter 6, for example, does not minimize necessary transmissive skills, such as reading. What it does demonstrate, as Dewey so brilliantly wrote, is that "interest and effort" in education are reciprocal, not antagonistic, propensities of human learning. To promote this kind of reciprocity is never easy, to be sure—certainly not if, by the time typical students reach high school, they have become miseducated and hence unmotivated both by the egg-crate curriculum and by ordained requirements of learning.

The disillusioned and therefore innovated curriculum is, by contrast, geared at every stage to the very real experience of learners—no matter at what age. Consequently, it means that a substantial part of the school program occurs, not in the formal classroom, but in the local, regional, national, and ultimately international community. It means that teachers are effectively trained anthropologically and sociologically as well as psychologically, and hence that both they and students engage in continuous, expertly directed involvement all the way from nearby ghetto life to fairly distant foreign cultures. It means that the surrounding natural and social environment is constantly utilized as a boundless resource of learning. Finally, it means a freshly designed model of the "community school"—not the caricature we now often hear about but a school that provides wide, busy, *two-way avenues*, equally traveled in both directions by learners on the adult level and by children of nursery-school age and upward.

9. This illusion, please recall from Chapter 1, is the hoary one of the alleged evils of economic support and federal control of education. We have already pretty well exploded the myth of local and state financial adequacy for education. But we have hardly begun to think through a political philosophy sufficiently updated to cognize not only that enormously strengthened federal support is necessary but that carefully formulated practices of federal authority are needed as well.

Thus, the pertinent issue is not whether we can or should artificially dichotomize federal support and control. Rather, the issue is whether such control is or could be democratically and authentically expressive of majority will. Here, of course, power becomes central. Behind it is the question of whether any nation can still be constructed with the locus of power genuinely centered in that majority. I do not believe that this will be possible until and unless the present network of concentrated power is superseded by patterns of modern democratic socialization geared to the maximum needs of the citizenry as a whole. By maximum needs, I mean, of course, scientifically established standards of health, nourishment, housing, and education; but more than this: access to the resources of art, recreation, travel, communication, and all other resources thus far denied to vast numbers of people across the globe, including many Americans.

Simultaneously, "decentralized" control counterbalanced with federal control becomes a concomitant principle—not at all for the sake of new forms of authority that could be just as disillusioning as the old, but for the sake of cooperatively developed community plans and tasks. Thereby parents, students, and teachers learn to join in open, unrestricted dialogue and to arrive as patiently as possible at tenable, functioning, and self-correcting guides of operation.

These samples of controversial political theory themselves merely illustrate the meaning of a modernized and revitalized curriculum—a curriculum focused on the pressing, concrete problems of mankind and subjected to the most searching questions and criticisms that can be raised in the adventure of teaching and learning.

10. The illusion of nationalism, as exemplified by the truncated programs of UNESCO, compels us to pay far more explicit attention to power as an end as well as to power as means. It is hoped, even so, that power as an end is at least implicit in what has been said about means—in, for example, the as yet only partially, crudely articulated goals of student power and black power.

Nevertheless, an acute demand arises in education for prolonged attention to such goals—above all, to a realizable world order. Here is a theme demanding more patient, more probing diagnosis and prognosis than any other single problem of our time.

The pity is that, to an alarming extent, the means and ends of a viable community of nations are neglected by most educators. One hears, to be sure, occasional lip-service paid to the United Nations. But what is actually required is vastly more than this: it is that the problems and expectations of mankind as a whole should become nothing less than the core of *every* curriculum, beginning in its own terms of maturation at the kindergarten level and extending all the way to the college and adult levels.

Here surely is a captivating goal in itself. Therefore it compels us to utilize and to discover all that we can about the earth's resources, about population control, about the dangers and promises of technology, about the deep-seated conflicts that invade political-economic struggles, and certainly about similar as well as dissimilar value patterns of cross-cultural ethnic and racial clusterings. It is a goal that can provide direction as no patchwork remedies of the curriculum can possibly provide; that can replace the emptiness and sterility of much of the present program; that can arouse the younger generation (in partnership with the older) to seek and express its own significance and purpose; and finally that can strive for a UNESCO with authority to construct a planctary, democratically directed program of education.

Like the preceding nine illusions, the disillusion of nationalism is not to be interpreted, therefore, in a merely negative sense. The corollary of this disillusion can be the positive and universal affirmation of a worldwide humanity, of vibrant purposes that could and should transcend our long overworked illusions.

5. The Quality of Intellectual Discipline in America

Of the seven words in the title of this chapter, only three are beyond controversy. They are: "the," "of," and "in." All four of the remaining words are fraught with debatable meanings. They are: "quality," "intellectual," "discipline," and "America."

The last of these four deserves comment first. In a book published over thirty years ago, the late Alexander Meiklejohn asked *What Does America Mean?* Today his question is even more disturbing, for the image of America has become blurred and tarnished in the eyes of the world.

The state of education in general and of intellectual discipline in particular is, moreover, acutely symptomatic of this condition. Perhaps it is truistic to reassert that education—no matter what its specific structures, programs, or objectives—invariably and everywhere serves a double function: one to reinforce, the other to reshape the beliefs and habits of our culture. But it is hardly truistic to re-emphasize that the conflicts and other troubles endemic to American life as a whole are also endemic to education. Only witness once again the extraordinary shift among growing minorities of students from the preceding fashion of aloofness to their current mood of volcanic activity. Witness, too, the almost unprecedented militancy of tens of thousands of teachers who have been demanding rights and rewards that they hold to be commensurate with their services.

These instances could be easily compounded. But the point I wish to underscore is evident enough: my subject must not be sheltered in the groves of academe. Rather, it must be examined within the context of what contemporary America means and of the explosive world situation with which America is entangled.

Let us turn, accordingly, to each of the remaining symbols of controversy. "Quality" in intellectual discipline, for example, is far more difficult to characterize than one might suppose if one equated it to any considerable degree with "quantity." Everyone is aware of the skyrocketing curve of education through high school, college, and now all the way through the doctoral degree. It is also evident that quantitative standards of academic achievement and promotion have risen—a consequence, in part, of the more and more rigidly selective admission to upper levels of learning; in part, also, of the increased emphasis on subjects that lend themselves to precision of performance. Recall the recent sweeping changes in "new math" curricula widely adopted by elementary schools, or the modernized physics courses in high schools. On the graduate level, too, professions specializing in rigorous research have made prodigious advances—most dramatically, no doubt, in the constant application of the exact sciences, to the transformation of our automating industrial complex, but also to revolutionary systems of communication and transportation that already extend fantastically beyond man's earthbound existence.

And yet, impressive though the expansion of these knowledges and skills surely is, we should be suspicious of any dogmatic pronouncement that a higher or richer quality of intellectual discipline is the inevitable consequence of such expansion. Surely, quality in any sense germane to this discussion must connote criteria of judgment not determined by quantity alone. Quality, in other words, connotes judgments as to what is of *most worth* in education. Therefore, it cannot possibly be attributed exclusively either to the amounts of education, however extensive, or to its measured products, however awesome.

In the light of current policies and behavior, does American education reveal awareness of this crucial distinction? I contend that it does not. Recalling again the perennial readiness of educational institutions (above all, readiness to respond to technological imperatives), one may express alarm over certain trends that becloud any clear delineation of moral criteria of quality as superior to amoral, and sometimes immoral, criteria of quantity.

Allow me to support this contention with a series of examples. One familiar to all of us is the demand of industry and government for a great range of expertise—a demand so voracious that the so-called brain drain from abroad has already approached scandalous proportions. Nor are high-stratum experts the only ones sought after; opportunities are open to millions of citizens who are able to perform jobs demanding skills ranging from fairly modest mechanical proficiency to extremely complex engineering.

No wonder that the curricula of representative high schools and colleges have become increasingly weighted with subjects and skills geared to our technologized culture. No wonder, either, that other spheres of the curriculum have not maintained comparable pace. Signs of improvement in these spheres are discernible, to be sure. Yet if we survey the contents of curricula across the nation we find that the proportions of time and budget devoted to qualitative learnings in, say, music, painting, poetry, drama, and dance are paltry indeed compared with the physical and biological sciences. So, too, social studies are typically lower in standards of content and practice.

On more sophisticated academic planes, much the same appraisal applies to such sciences of man as psychology, sociology, political science. One is struck by a double phenomenon: the comparatively meager backing that these human sciences receive in federal funding, and the frequency with which they resort to statistical and other meticulous forms of research in their apparent eagerness to emulate the natural sciences.

Another example of the proliferation of quantity as the primary criterion of quality is the zealous promotion of what has come to be popularly described as "educational hardware." Within less than half a decade, huge mergers have been launched between electronics corporations and the so-called software publishing industry. Their aim is no secret: to capture the burgeoning educational market with a vast gadgetry of cybernetic inventions, audiovisual labyrinths, and every other ingenious device that can be designed to "programmatize" and mechanize the process of learning and teaching.

It would be foolish to condemn this profitable giant enterprise. By comparison with the cumbersome, wasteful procedures of formal schooling that have hitherto been commonplace, automation *can* provide more efficient means by which to acquire various kinds of knowledge and skills. But what should trouble us about the period directly ahead is not whether to reject these devices, even if we could. Rather, the issue is whether they will, on the one hand, succeed in turning classrooms into conveyor-belt and pushbutton learning factories or, on the other hand, release time and energy on all levels of education for vastly more exciting learning in quality—for originality and creativity in the art studio as well as in the science laboratory, for continuous environmental experience, and, above all, for rich, close association between individual teacher and individual student.

Still another instance of the powerful role of quantification draws us closer to the third of our controversial terms: "intellectual." I refer to the contemporary state of philosophy—a state that becomes directly relevant to our concern if we are willing to regard philosophy (somewhat as we have implied for education) less in strictly academic terms than as the intellectual expression and interpretation of deeper meanings of culture.

Now, philosophy in America has come in recent years to pay far more attention to one historic division of its discipline than to any other—so much so, indeed, that an impressive proportion of our younger philosophers seem to regard all other divisions, such as the philosophy of art or religion, as largely if not entirely outmoded. I refer, of course, to the currently fashionable philosophy of science, and particularly to schools of thought familiarly labeled logical empiricism or philosophic analysis.

It thus should be hardly surprising if most philosophic analysts become impatient with, if not contemptuous toward, criteria of quality that cannot be treated according to the canons of logical precision. Many such criteria, after all, presuppose a life of values—and values are frequently regarded as arbitrary or otherwise merely personalized kinds of experience, of little "intellectual" worth because they are incapable of scientific verification.

If this picture of American philosophy today seems

overdrawn, my principal contention is not: the main thrust of contemporary scientific philosophy is entirely harmonious with the over-all thrust of our precision-minded culture. Therefore, it tends to reinforce the technological pressures exerted upon academic achievement. And it becomes perhaps an unwitting salesman for the "educational hardware" corporations, an adjunct to the huge promotion campaigns already being waged under the banner of higher academic standards.

We can well understand, then, not only why the current fad of the philosophy of education likewise appears to be an exercise in scientific-analytic applications to problems of, say, learning or teaching, but also why it is equally inclined to subordinate, if not repudiate, alternative meanings of the "intellectual" sphere. According to the classical tradition of education, for example, "intellect" is frequently allied with the supreme "faculty of reason"—the primary purpose being to cultivate "reason" to maximum human potentialities. Culturally speaking, this tradition is peremptorily dismissed by scientific-analytic philosophers of education, just as it is by their academic prototypes in the exact sciences: for both, "intellectual" performances are no longer determinable by criteria of human "worth" in the senses once advocated by Plato and Aristotle but, rather, by performances ultimately as testable and empirically acceptable as any other phenomena of objective nature.

The core meaning of the term "intellectual," whether conceived in the analytical or the classical sense, could be expressed by still further philosophies of education, but I am able to mention only one other that reveals a qualified compatibility with either of these senses yet proves its own distinctive and exceptional influence.

The key to this position is detected in such terms as "organismic" or "holistic"—terms leading to a conception of human nature as dynamic, multifaceted experience. There-

by, the "intellectual" sphere is no longer regarded either as
some sort of autonomous faculty or as any exactly determinable process, but, rather, as integrated throughout with
the emotional and social fabric of that experience. In sim-
plest terms, life is a whole, and so, rightly understood, is
education.

Such a viewpoint of the expansive role of the "intellectual" has recently been strengthened and supplemented, not
always eagerly, to be sure, by the still young and far from
unified field of psychoanalysis. The educable individual is
pictured as a pattern of drives and expectations that function beneath and beyond his "conscious," hence exclusively
"intellectual" or "rational," characteristics. A familiar paradox thus emerges: the "intellectual" life becomes successful only as it detects its own limitations. This is not to
suggest that the task of the psychiatrist, and certainly not
of the educator, is to deny the importance of consciousness;
it is to insist upon the power of and control over man's
unconscious and subconscious nature. For without this
exceedingly strenuous effort, man can never become effectively conscious at all.

Nevertheless, I question whether the sort of flexible,
dynamic, and holistic philosophy to which I am referring,
and to which I shall pay further attention especially in
Chapter 7, has succeeded thus far in prevailing over
any large segment of American education. To be sure,
some advances have been quite impressive, particularly during the period extending roughly from the 1920's to the
1950's. Today, too, it remains sporadic in its influence. But
when we are willing to adjudge education as an institutional
surrogate of culture, we find substantial evidence that this
philosophy has at least temporarily retreated rather than
advanced during the current period of educational theory
or practice.

As for the professional preparation of teachers, our most severe opponents of colleges of education have oftener than not circumvented the essential problem of the "intellectual." For what these opponents have urged instead rarely amounts to much more than the perpetuation of subject matters and the command of skills harmonious with conventional orders—hence it is often evaluated by the same quantified standards that they, too, usually admire. Although their foremost complaint, according to such criteria, is that teacher preparation is too often adulterated or cheapened, they seldom offer viable alternatives, if only because their own philosophies of education are vaguely assumed rather than critically assessed.

Thus we reach our fourth debatable term: "discipline." And once more the focal question is: What does this term actually mean?

To elevate standards of physics or mathematics or other "basic" subjects is obviously to endorse the strict mastery demanded. But do we settle much if anything by this endorsement? Granted that teacher education, for one, too frequently encourages "anti-intellectualism" in its failure to respect or to achieve high standards of scholarship, are there no less conventional meanings of "discipline" than this?

One of several additional meanings is frequently ignored, not only by American education, but by Western culture as a whole. I refer to the subtle conception of subjectively personal "discipline" embraced and practiced by schools of philosophy of the East—Zen Buddhism being among the most prominent. To a shocking extent, Americans remain immune to the rich contributions that these philosophies could offer to human well-being. Consider, by comparison, how one of the few American philosophers sensitive to Eastern thought is able to suggest an analogy with the paradox to which I have already referred—the psychiatric view of consciousness. Says E. A. Burtt:

> Western thinkers have been the pioneers in realizing the freedom that man can achieve through reason, while the Eastern sages have led the way in realizing the freedom that needs to be achieved . . . from the limitations of reason. . . . Man's primary need is freedom from the forces within himself. . . .[1]

"Discipline," in this meaning, points not only toward social control of institutions, such as technology, that enable men to function systematically together, but also toward control of each man within himself—a synthesis, as it were, of "outer" and "inner" freedom.

Another conception extends well beyond rigorously objectified, often coldly competitive, notions of discipline. This conception thus remains very much the exception rather than the rule in American classrooms—increasingly so as we follow their performances from early childhood education to the college years. I am speaking here of social discipline, defined as cooperative planning and participation in the learning-teaching process. By and large—again gladly granting some variations from customary practices— tens of thousands of students, especially in the large universities, are exposed to almost no teaching by their professors other than lecturing or demonstrating, and to no learning other than restating (often by means of IBM cards) what these professors or their textbooks and laboratory exercises have conveyed to them in the first place.

The discipline to which I am now referring derives, on the contrary, from what some social philosophers and social psychologists call "transactional learning"—learning that encourages continuous, critical, open communication and that eventuates in understandings different from, perhaps superior to, any understandings that either teachers or students have hitherto acquired. (The connections of this view with what I have earlier termed the "holistic" orientation and what I shall later term "psychocultural ethics" are, of course, intimate.)

Such a view of social discipline remains, nevertheless, a circumscribed one: it still functions primarily within or adjacent to the boundaries of school and college environments. Therefore a still further conception is now called for.

Here let us refer again to the phenomenon of student activism. If the American people are willing to confront the age in which they live, does not the younger generation deserve the privilege to confront it as well? And is not confrontation itself the expression of capabilities and expectations of learning to participate in the problems and tasks of immediate, perhaps still wider, communities?

That such an expression generates misgivings, even alarm, within the educational and political Establishment is only too apparent, particularly as student movements gain impressive influence throughout the world.

Yet some may question whether I am talking about *intellectual* discipline at all. Certainly not, in orthodox academic parlance. But certainly yes, if one is willing to consider more inclusive, defensible criteria. The social discipline of organized and purposeful involvement, however clumsy and at moments harsh, remains the democratic obligation of citizens in the best sense of that term. In this assertion I certainly do not condone those extremes of violence that succeed only in generating counterextremes of repression. But I do maintain that mature, legitimate, aggressive expressions of social discipline challenge all of us in education, and assuredly students, to share equitably in refurbishing educational structures, in redirecting educational processes—above all, in redesigning the most audacious, compelling purposes of which American and world cultures are capable.

To restate, then, our brief consideration of "discipline," not one but several meanings emerge. We *do* need higher standards of academic excellence that at times require quantified substantiation. But we need other kinds, too: the discipline of selfhood epitomized by the venerable insights of Eastern thought; the discipline of cooperative learning and teaching; and certainly, the discipline of active, responsible community experience.

That more conventional views remain by far more agreeable to both administrative and instructional echelons is obviously true. But it is also true that other views are gaining respect and influence. The proliferation of student energy in and dedication to antipoverty programs, for example, has been profoundly inspired by what some young people are sometimes learning from socially, politically, or culturally aware teachers.

Nor should we denigrate the considerable impact of formal and informal education, including television and other media of popular communication, on a still-wider scale; the awakening, however sluggish, of public awareness of the need for national support in behalf of the arts, such as theater and orchestra; the growing demands for fair housing, health services, old-age security, and better schools for all citizens; and, not least of all, the sharp dissent against regressive foreign policies and actions. These are impressive indeed.

No one would care to assert, surely, that the perplexities posed by our theme can be fully resolved—least of all in literally "black" or "white" terms. The character of American life is never reducible to simple equations. Nevertheless, one or two concluding judgments are warranted.

As long as we resort to convenient academic yardsticks, the question before us is simple enough to answer. "Intellectual discipline" *is* improving in America in the sense that education, as an indispensable servant of the most amazing technological advances of all time, is likewise improving. But by other, less tangible criteria, the answer is far from clear-cut. Thus "intellectual" proves to be a very complex conception, symbolizing as it does not one but several philosophies of human nature, together with the comparable ways that education relates to these philosophies. "Discipline," too, remains truncated in its meaning until stretched to include, not only both Western *and* Eastern perspectives, but the bipolarities of individual *and* social learning through direct, vigorous experience.

Obviously, we can still choose to justify and perpetuate "the quality of intellectual discipline in America" upon the comfortable assumptions of our past. But equally, we can choose to recognize that, with all their remarkable contributions, neither these assumptions nor their consequences are any longer sufficient—rather, that to the same degree that we accept and defend them, we also rationalize their obsolescences and accelerate their dangers.

I am not at all sure which of these two compelling choices will predominate. I am very sure that astute educational spokesmen will do their best, amid polite concessions, to persuade us that conventionality is by far the more rewarding, unconventionality by far the less.

But, in the last analysis, neither alternative alone will do. Each compels us to raise the solemn and baffling question to which I have merely alluded: How can education be invigorated and canalized in behalf, not merely or even primarily of swift technological advance, but of the peaceful fulfillment of man himself? Unless our intellectual powers now become disciplined to answer this question before all others, is there really any hope for America or, for that matter, for civilization as a whole?

6. Confronting the Values of Youth

In accordance with one traditional role of the philosopher, let us again begin with a set of premises. Some people, indeed, define philosophy as the discipline that attempts to examine and enunciate the "inarticulate major premises" upon which education and all other human enterprises rest.

First premise: *Problems of value are central to human life.* The question of the meaning of values, where they come from, and what their impact may be upon life is, in a very real sense, the most difficult and, at the same time, the most important that might be asked.

Another premise: *Values permeate all aspects of human existence.* They are not limited to a narrow sphere—for instance, to the personal or the psychological—but embrace all dimensions of individual and social life.

Still another premise: *These various dimensions of life*

are embodied in a series of institutions which may be de-picted as a series of overlapping circles: politics, economics, science, art, recreation, religion, the family, and, last but not least, education itself. Within each circle, we detect implicit and to some extent explicit valuational dimensions or—as some anthropologists prefer to call them—value orientations. In any case, none of these circles is immune to crucial problems of value.

Next premise: *Not only is each great institution perme-ated with value but, in our day at least, each one of them is permeated with complexities.* Not a single one, from poli-tics to the family and education, is free from instability and confusion. Life today is more controversial, indeed, than it has been at any time in the history of the human race. Some of the reasons for this situation are familiar enough. But we may be sure that none of them has been sufficient-ly explored.

Next premise: *The knowledge that is generated within each of these dimensions of human existence is burdened with conflict, and the causes of conflict are many*—so many that no one, even the most presumptuous, can claim to understand them fully.

Here I wish merely to illustrate. Although it is by no means a sufficient cause—for there are many causes behind this cause—consider the concept in social psychology called the "frustration-aggression complex," a concept which has itself undergone extended refinement since its original formulation.

In some of my own field research, I have found the complementary reaction of frustration causing aggression, and aggression in turn causing more frustration, to be one of the most fruitful of all explanations of human behavior. To throw the spotlight more directly on young people, it may be argued that if we are to interpret the painful dis-ruptions that innumerable youngsters are experiencing today, we shall have to utilize the frustration-aggression complex and other concepts much more extensively than we have done thus far.

Young people frequently *are* frustrated. Therefore, they often tend to act aggressively: their frustrations must somehow find an outlet. Juvenile delinquency, for example, is partly attributable to the fact that adolescents often discover no release for their dissatisfactions and denials other than antisocial behavior. And this behavior, in turn, feeds upon the confusions and bewilderments to which I have referred.

One or two more premises, please. Education, one of the great institutions in our simple model and surely by no means of least importance, is obligated to every one of the other institutions. To say that education lacks concern for one or another aspect of human existence is thus to confess that education fails to recognize the entire range of values that permeate these institutions.

Here it becomes useful to consider a familiar but important distinction—the distinction between "descriptive" and "normative" values. Although I shall consider this matter in a later chapter, let us here imagine how a sociologist might very simply describe values: "Here are the values that people actually reveal when we observe them. Here are the value patterns that boys and girls in Hartford, Connecticut, say, accept in their everyday behavior."

This *descriptive* investigation of values is necessary to any imaginative approach to value problems. Nevertheless, to an extraordinary and appalling extent, behavioral scientists have too often skirted factors of value central to the major institutions of culture. The descriptive study of values both within cultures and between cultures, through cross-cultural research, is one of the most neglected of all social-science tasks.

But this, too, is far from enough. The other fundamental approach to problems of value is *normative*. In essence, this approach is concerned with justifying the desirability of values to which we not only do but also should subscribe. The question of what values we should hold thus becomes a question of normative axiology, to borrow another technical term. It is that branch of philosophy concerned with whatever desirable norms may be justified on the most reliable grounds available to us. The question, accordingly, of how, if at all, we can arrive at judgments about what we should hold to be good or desirable or beautiful thus becomes the other half of the axiological equation.

A final premise, then, relates to all others, yet it deserves even more attention. In my view, *education, to a very great extent, is failing in its concern for ethical aspects of the major institutions of culture.* If this is so, then it follows that education also fails to distinguish sufficiently between, or to manifest direct, explicit, systematic, patient concern for, the two primary phases of value—the descriptive and the normative.

Still, it would be foolish to generalize without qualification. Many individual teachers (mostly unsung) are poignantly concerned with both the descriptive and normative values of their children. By and large, nevertheless, I fail to find that American educators—or, for that matter, the educators of other countries where I have studied—are in any adequate way directing themselves to crucial questions that the valuational dimensions of every institution of human life now generate.

Let us return, then, to the several institutions, which were merely named, and try to exemplify the contention that each of them is fraught with conflict and confusion.

Begin with the area of politics. I am not referring at the moment to internal political conflicts within the United

States (although these are severe enough) but to profound implications of value inherent in the meaning of loyalty to our nation. Now, it is true that public schools do sometimes talk about this issue. Even so, all the evidence that I have seen points toward the conclusion that many young people are threatened by a kind of political schizophrenia with regard to whether their primary loyalty should lie with the country in which they live or with some kind of transnational concept, not merely to the United Nations, but to a union of democracies organized, for example, in the way that the World Federalists propose.

What we in education are doing is, in effect, to bring up a generation of young people who are bewildered over where their allegiance really lies. One of our tasks, therefore, is to confront the dilemma involved in national citizenship as a descriptive value, on the one hand, and international loyalty as a normative value, on the other.

To point up the question differently, can we hold, realistically speaking, both loyalties at the same time? I believe that we can—and must. I also fear, however, that our schools are doing very little to help the typical youngster think through this dilemma. Yet unless it *is* thought through, I have no doubt whatever that we are heading toward the most fearful danger.

Instead, then, of pushing the value of loyalty over to the edge of the curriculum, should we not seriously consider what to take *out* of the curriculum in order to put this *in?* Only too frequently I meet superintendents of schools and principals who say, "Oh, some of your ideas sound all right, but we just don't have room to turn them into practice." Well, here too is a problem of values, is it not? The crucial question is what is *most important* to the lives of young people. Everything cannot be equally important.

I, for one, would be glad to replace a very substantial share of the present junior and senior high-school curricu-

lum with problems far more urgent to human beings today than those treated in most conventional courses. The
value of loyalty is one of these problems.

To select another example, we know perfectly well that
religion has played and continues to play powerful roles in
the life of man. But because of our tradition of separation
of church and state, public schools in America have been
understandably reluctant to help young people develop a
mature stance toward the central place of the great religions
in modern civilization. Thus they have been reluctant to
approach values in the explicit context of religious experience.

Since the whole of Part III is devoted to this question,
I shall say here only that the opportunity for young people
to consider the meaning of this experience as embodied in
an institution embracing not merely Christianity or Judaism but Buddhism, Mohammedanism, Humanism, and
other nontheistic as well as theistic views of religion, is a
magnificent one. So far as I know, our public schools have
almost totally avoided this opportunity.

A further instance is drawn from the innermost circle
of institutions. Few would deny that the family has been
undergoing upheaval. We know that customary patterns
of family living have fluctuated markedly under the development of technology and urbanism. We also know that
profound changes are consequently taking place in the
relations of the sexes. Yet, just as religion remains predominantly a taboo subject, and just as frank controversy
involving, say, radical political positions is frequently avoided or softpedalled in the public schools, so too are
anxieties generated by the "sexual revolution" rarely dealt
with by educators. Here, too, I propose that this issue must
be faced forthrightly.

But in one respect the difficulty can be resolved simply.
If we believe that the obligation of education is to concern

itself only with matters so innocuous that they never arouse any of the pressure groups constantly on the schools' doorstep—if, in short, we say that education had better avoid controversy and play it safe—then we are not going to deal squarely with the ethics of sexual behavior.

Certainly few will disagree that children are still learning, however. Almost from birth, consciously or not, they are learning about sex every day in the week. All of us did and do, too. But the relevant question is, what kind of learning really takes place?

Here one is reminded of a term that Dewey insightfully used: "miseducative learning." Many kinds of learning are possible—some constructive, intelligent, rational; others destructive, ignorant, irrational. Since to a great extent the schools have abrogated their responsibility for the often agonizing ethical choices faced by youth caught up by the transformation in sexual mores, by default they have supported miseducative learning in this crucial area of human life.

Now may I submit for your critical reaction a set of targets—normative targets—for the schools of America? By "schools" I mean, of course, not merely formal institutions but the entire educative enterprise, including adult education such as occurs in, say, labor unions, churches, and organizations of minority groups. In a broad cultural sense, how might "schools" tackle their multiple problems of value?

The kind of education that is willing to deal with *all* such problems, not just some of them, will recognize that all of the several spheres or institutions of human life are the responsibility of education, from the kindergarten to beyond the college and university. These institutions then are the first target of the curriculum—both the formal curriculum and the informal learnings of extracurricular and community programs.

I re-emphasize that each sphere is thoroughly controversial, for nothing significant involving human life today is *not* controversial. Indeed, I defy you to think of a single area of knowledge, even the so-called quantitative sciences, such as physics and chemistry, that is not now profoundly debatable—debatable in the sense that the knowledge explosion has forced us to re-examine inherited models, from the Newtonian model of traditional physics to outmoded family patterns once suitable to an agrarian age.

But our purpose is surely not to develop mere skeptics. Nor is it to aggravate the disease of alienation rampant among young people. Our purpose, rather, is to join with them in facing the world as it actually is—a world of revolutionary change through which, and only through which, they and we may strive toward resolution of controversy in terms of a life-affirming pattern of existence.

The preceding remark suggests our next target. How can we move from study of the controversial nature of human life to critical study of its valuational dimensions—dimensions at once descriptive and normative? The descriptive level is much easier in a way, of course. Few people complain if, for example, an anthropologist enters a particular culture and studies its valuational patterns objectively. But anthropologists themselves often cringe whenever someone attempts to infer normative judgments from their descriptive studies. As suggested above, many social scientists try to avoid normative value judgments altogether.

But I do not speak here primarily as a social scientist. Admittedly, it may be easier for a philosopher to insist (in education at least) that we cannot possibly avoid shifting from exclusively descriptive studies of values toward normative levels of human experience. Yet how does it become legitimate to shift toward these levels?

Let me anticipate the next chapter by saying that the concept of value I have found especially fruitful in answering this difficult question is *social-self-realization*. This, to be sure, is an awkward term. But it becomes essential in order to counterbalance the implication of Abraham Maslow and other scholars who tempt us to understress the social dimensions of value. *Self*-actualization, Maslow's own preferred term, is basically a psychological concept; thus it detracts from concern for the sociological—in this case, for *social*-actualization.

The norm that should now be sought and developed is, then, bipolar. Of course, the individual seeks to fulfill his own personality. But each of us is integrally related to other human beings who likewise seek fulfillment. In short, each of us holds membership, deliberately or not, in collective arrangements extending all the way from the nuclear family to racial, religious, political, and other institutional values that eventually become planetary in scope.

The key here is *commitment*. Social-self-realization, for those who accept it, *is* a commitment. But until young people can internalize the affective as well as the cognitive meanings of this supreme value, they are likely to suffer (as many of them are already suffering) from their lack of purposeful affirmation and dedication. The need to discover and to believe in personal-social norms that are defensible scientifically, emotionally, and aesthetically has become inescapable.

People often talk today about conformity versus nonconformity. A few years ago, I was one of those who complained volubly about how "conformist" our high-school and college students appeared to be. Since the eruption of countless student "riots," many people are complaining about altogether too much nonconformity. Actually, however, the alternative is not a return to conformity; it is commitment to the guiding star of social-self-realization—a commitment relevant to peoples of all nations, all races, and all religions, no matter where you find them.

To provide education with depths of meaning for this encompassing value is, I maintain, essential. Moreover, as this value becomes increasingly translated into institutional experience, it provides infinite opportunity to examine critically and to express one's own distinctive values.

But if we are to move from our first target, which asks us to deal honestly with all areas of controversy, including values, to our second target, to a constructive expression of values that can become an overarching normative goal, then we require a thorough overhauling of the curriculum of the schools and colleges. If we are willing to consider the contention that man is passing through a time of upheaval unique in the history of his species, and if we are willing to admit, further, that the revolutions of our century produce controversy about every one of the institutions of human life—then we should also be willing to ask whether we are not selling our young people very short by insisting on subjects, grades, and other requirements that have scant significance for a large percentage of them.

Yes, of course, let us admire the "new math" and "new physics" even if we may seriously question the emphasis so abundantly given to them. Nevertheless, as the father of a teen-age daughter, I find myself wondering to what extent and to what depth these subjects help Kristin to learn about the kind of world into which she is now being inducted. Her "above-average" high school is chiefly concerned with subjects that almost certainly guarantee admission into some college. But what else do they guarantee? What do they communicate to her as a potential young citizen growing up amid social and political explosions, upsetting religious skepticism, liberalizing sexual conduct, dislocating ecologies and technologies? Above all, to what extent is such an education preparing Kristin to analyze her own mutations—mutations of value interwoven throughout with these cultural upheavals?

I fear that the curriculum to which she and countless others are subjected is fast becoming an immoral curriculum. True, one of the areas implicit in our model of over-lapping institutions receives attention. This is the institution of politics. A little attention is also being devoted to some of the remarkable transformations taking place in the arts. The bulk of Kristin's time in school, nevertheless, is devoted to courses familiar to both her parents. Almost no one seems to be explicitly, or even implicitly, concerned to search with her for any conceivable fruitful relationships that might prevail between each neat little block of knowledge.

For this reason alone, the redesigning of typical curricula is long overdue. The central, flexible focus of such redesigning is the fascinating, utterly astonishing world of modern man-in-culture. Whatever Kristin may be studying, whether science or history or math, the specific discipline should be blended into dynamic wholes. For she should be experiencing a curriculum in which man-in-culture is the core of every subject and every teacher is far more concerned to make sure this is so than to see that she will climb still one more rung of the educational (hence the status) ladder.

During one memorable discussion period at a conference of teachers, a written question reached me: "But how can you possibly expect me, as a typing teacher, to be concerned with some of the ideas you are talking about? My assignment is specific—to teach my kids to write good business letters." Well, surely, a curriculum organized about the guidelines I have proposed would open boundless opportunities for the typing teacher to work closely with the literature teacher, the social-studies teacher, the science teacher. Typing, like any other skill, would become one further means by which children learn to express themselves more clearly, interestingly, and idiosyncratically in every other area of learning. The point is all too familiar. Yet often, the average teacher prefers to treat his or her specialty as a sovereign domain, with little if any regard for what children could be learning cooperatively in other domains.

The next target has to do with methodology. Although I am far from expert in the science or art of learning-teaching, I do wish to suggest one supreme methodological principle. Let us call it *involvement*.

This is not to propose an occasional field excursion that begins in the morning and ends in the afternoon. This *is* to propose a *continuing program* in which each learner, whether on the elementary or the secondary level, spends at least a quarter of his time utilizing the community as a classroom—every aspect of the community, moreover, as embraced by every one of its institutions.

Despite lip-service, we have made paltry progress in this direction thus far. I am aware of some of the obstacles (assuring safe, quick transportation is only one). But I also know from observation that, if we are sufficiently concerned, these obstacles can be overcome. And when they *are* overcome there is nothing more exciting, more rewarding, than the kind of adventures I am here urging. Surely, if we have never learned anything else from the great progressivists in educational philosophy, we must have learned this.

As a fellow-learner I, too, try often to engage in such involvement. In a single course in educational anthropology, my students and I have entered annually into cultures and subcultures not only throughout New England itself but as far away as the French Canadian communities of

Quebec, the Amish neighborhoods of Pennsylvania, and the traditionally Hispanic culture of Puerto Rico. In each case, we have tried to practice cautiously with anthropological tools, such as acculturation. Certainly in no case have we claimed to understand more than our circumscribed contacts justify. Yet, in every case, involvement has meant not just talking *about* the experience of ethnic, racial, class, religious, or other patterns of cultural life, but *having* such experience.

In the case of Puerto Rico, to recall but one venture, I am convinced that my students and I, who together had been reading about that remarkable island for many weeks, are now more knowledgeable and appreciative than we could possibly have become through the exclusively verbalized learning still so characteristic of school and college programs.

And now our final target: values are not merely embodied in everyday events; they are also complex philosophic problems.

It is said that somebody once remarked to Albert Einstein, "Professor Einstein, you often seem to be keenly interested in political questions. Why didn't you ever consider becoming a political scientist?" Einstein reportedly smiled and answered, "My friend, political science is infinitely more difficult than physics!" And no wonder, if we note that political science is one of the behavioral sciences fraught with problems of human value.

But just because these problems *are* difficult, we cannot afford in our concern with youth to ignore their philosophic aspects. Here at least two approaches deserve our consideration. One includes opportunities for teacher-training institutions: the time should soon come when no teacher will graduate from a college of education without having engaged in probing examination of important developments within the branch of philosophy called axiology. Nor is this objective at all impossible; rather, it is a matter of assuring that axiology is both available and relevant by means of teachers professionally competent to deal with it.

But value studies can be introduced in the public schools as well. In Japan, for example, students in the public schools are expected to study ethical concepts and problems as a regular part of the curriculum. This requirement, however strange it may seem to Americans, is an idea that works, although far from perfectly. Japanese educators make countless mistakes and are highly critical of what they call "moral education." Some of them are aware, too, of the danger of inculcating the teacher's own values or the dominant political party's values. Yet, despite the hazards involved, it is my impression that the Japanese are pioneers in approaching the values of their own young people as well as the values of other peoples and other cultures.

Here, then, are my normative targets. Surely they require further discussion and modification. I take for granted that you will disagree with some of them. For is this not still another involvement that is requisite to the study of values on the part of all who function as students, teachers, and citizens?

The methodological bridge of the generation gap may well test our eagerness to join with young people in reciprocal involvement with the values of life. These are the girders, after all, of man-in-culture.

7. Creative Ethics for Educational Leadership

        In this chapter, I propose to continue the discussion of ethics in education as it bears still more fundamentally upon tasks of leadership.

The crucial point is that contemporary educational leaders—principals, superintendents, deans, college presidents, and others—today face a unique occasion. It has occurred to many of them, apparently rather suddenly, that comfortable, routine performances will no longer do. The compounded crisis of our own time, to which I have been referring throughout these pages, infuses and is infused by the crisis in education itself. Educational leaders, accordingly, have no choice but to reassess their own responsibilities, roles, and tasks and to reconsider with all their capacity what they must do if they are not to be repudiated by the burgeoning forces of change both within and without their own institutions.

Thus we are brought back to the crisis in ethics. I do not refer merely to the poignant questions of moral conduct, particularly to conflicts in sexual behavior among the younger generation. I refer also to problems of ethics that now preoccupy formal philosophy, particularly that major division of philosophy known as axiology—the interpretation of criteria of values. To read many of the treatises on this subject might lead one to suppose that professional philosophers are concerned only remotely, if at all, with the connection between burning questions of everyday life, such as sexual behavior, and their own intellectual preoccupations. Nevertheless, let us assume that these connections must exist somewhere, however tenuously, and that philosophy still reflects, however tangentially, the more pervasive conditions of the wider cultures which in the past it has sought to interpret and to serve.

One place to begin, if educational leaders are to take their novel obligations seriously, is with developments characteristic of ethical theory today. To confront these developments is, of course, a very large task made even more difficult by the fact that the professional preparation of educational administrators has frequently provided little more than fleeting attention to the substance and relevance of axiology. To grind one of my own favorite axes, one of the glaring weaknesses in both undergraduate and graduate programs of education is their casual and superficial treatment of the philosophic foundations of this institution—a weakness that surely contributes to the current difficulties of the profession in reducing its practitioners' ethical bewilderments.

Suppose that educational leaders thus far agree. If so, they face the difficulty implied by an earlier comment upon the state of axiology. For, if it is true that many professional axiologists seem to be extraordinarily immune to the chronic state of our human condition, and if it is equally true that some professional educators confess an almost desperate need to re-examine and clarify the axiological assumptions of their demanding roles, how is it possible to bridge the two spheres of concern? How, more precisely, can the best thinking that we can discover in the discipline of ethics be brought into communication with and eventually to fruitful action by educational leaders themselves?

A promising way to confront this dilemma is to consider three large questions. First, what typical concerns of contemporary philosophers of ethics may have special relevance for educational leaders? Second, if these concerns prove inadequate, is there some viable alternative that may conceivably have still greater relevance? And third, in the light of the current crisis (please remember that this provides background for our entire discussion), what ethical priorities could challenge educational leaders toward working strategies and policies?

Let us turn to the first question. Notwithstanding the lofty posture of too many philosophers today, what can we learn from them that may have useful bearings upon the ethical tasks of educational leaders? Parenthetically, it may be said that, certainly in America and to a considerable extent in Europe, the old categories of traditional philosophy are often regarded as obsolete. These old doctrines— idealism and realism, for example—are still common in conventional philosophic parlance, but they have less and less credulity. In their place, two points of view, both mentioned earlier, have recently generated interest. They may be called *linguistic analysis* and *existentialism*, although terminology, methodology, and foci of interest vary considerably within each point of view. Neither is by any means limited to axiological questions. But each seriously attempts to throw light upon these questions.

One might inquire at some length how these two positions happen to have grown to such stature during, roughly, the brief period between World War II and today. The answer, I think, is not to be found merely or even primarily in their formal character, but rather in the cultural milieu that has produced them. Unfortunately, this is a very large proposition which I cannot hope to examine here. Let me say only this: in very different ways, both linguistic analysis and existentialism respond to what they consider to be a breakdown not merely of traditional thought but, in some respects, of historic interpretations of Western civilization itself. Very broadly, linguistic analysis and its more venerable compatriots (notably logical positivism and logical empiricism) attempt to confront problems of ethics, as they do problems of other kinds, by analyzing objectively and neutrally whatever meanings are revealed by the language in which these meanings are couched. The other position, existentialism, is in one sense quite opposite. Whereas the first position is, as it were, unemotional and objective, the second often gives the impression of being deliberately emotional and subjective.

Of course, any generalization is bound to prove simplistic. Yet it cannot be denied that linguistic analysis and existentialism frequently appear to be polarized. An entire treatise, indeed, could be written on the disturbing cultural events that could have generated such hostile interpretations of man's philosophic role in modern life.

But turn to the more direct concern of what linguistic or philosophic analysis is trying to tell us that may have significance for ethics in education. Please note that we are engaging now in an exercise in *applied* philosophy: we want to make these apparently abstruse ideas work for us. But we have to be a little patient, too.

The linguistic analyst is responsible for at least two important contributions. One is his insistence upon precision of meaning. Therefore he tends to be unusually critical of educators, because he is likely to regard us as about as fuzzy a bunch of professionals as one could find anywhere. We feel free to use such ethical terms as "democracy," "the good life," "felt needs," the "dignity of personality." But we seldom define a single one of them satisfactorily.

Linguistic analysts have, indeed, recently sharpened educational theory to a considerable degree. We are indebted to Professors Kingsley Price, of Johns Hopkins University, and Israel Scheffler, of Harvard University, among others, for their insistence that we must know what we are talking about—and not least when we are talking about ethical questions in education.

The other contribution is more difficult, although the preceding one is difficult enough. It compels us to clarify further the difference between what was termed, in Chapter 6, "descriptive" and "normative" judgments. Descriptive judgments, sometimes called propositional judgments, appear to be very simple. They are judgments about fact. Take an ordinary drinking glass: it consists of certain chemical components that can be exactly described and may contain water, also describable chemically. But there are other kinds of judgment, which have to do with prescribing or judging a given situation as better (or worse) than another. The complementary term, although again others may be substituted, is therefore *normative*—judgments of what ought to be as compared with judgments of what is. If I say, for instance: "I should drink this glass of water because I'd feel better if I did," then, strictly speaking, I am making a prescriptive judgment; I am not merely describing the fact that I do drink the water. The logical or linguistic analyst has helped us to understand that much too often we jump illegitimately from the one judgment to the other; that is, we assume that because we are depicting a situation, it must therefore be a worthy situation. Sometimes this kind of jump also exposes the "naturalistic fallacy" of assuming that an event justifies our approval simply by virtue of its existence as a fact or experience of nature.

The term "desirable" sharpens the central point. Sexuality, for example, certainly is a norm as well as a fact. Educational leaders, including superintendents of schools, are frequently concerned about the unprecedented amount of sexual experimentation among American high-school students. We are all aware of the facts, but the axiological problem is not so evident: How can we proceed from the propositional judgment that people do have the desire for sexual experience, as they have the desire to drink water, to the judgment that it is as "right" to have sexual experiences as it is to drink water? The ancient ethical dilemma of desire and desirability here seems to be as acute as ever.

How do linguistic analysts resolve the dilemma? Their answers, partly because they themselves are in constant debate with one another, have rarely proved satisfying even to them. By and large, however (and again I must warn of the hazards of generalization), the analyst almost always concludes that there is no way, logically speaking, to justify prescriptive or normative judgments. One may offer them freely enough in the ordinary experience of every day, but to justify them in the way that one justifies propositional judgments is an entirely different matter.

Let me share one example. In a paper presented before a symposium on the philosophy of science, Professor Michael Martin, a brilliant young linguistic analyst, discusses certain philosophic problems of research methodology in anthropology. In dealing with the proliferating variables that abound in any science of man, and certainly in anthropology, the question of meanings becomes entangled in imprecise language and logically untenable assertions. The so-called methods of anthropology thus prove much too loose, much too vague. This paragraph brings out one of Professor Martin's chief contentions:

> It may be true that nowadays part of the ethical creed of the anthropological profession is humanitarianism and that part of this humanitarian attitude may be a sympathetic and tolerant attitude toward the community studied; that anthropologists are expected to be understanding toward the people they study. It must be stressed that however strong this commitment . . . and however justified it is on ethical grounds, there is no logical connection between this ethical posture and factual understanding of a community.[1]

So if an anthropologist in the field goes on to say, "I'd like to help you. I want you to become better people," this may be admirable enough "on ethical grounds" (whatever these are supposed to be), but let us not confuse them with "factual understanding," for there is "no logical connection" between the two. The consequence is that according to the linguistic analyst you and I, too, are likely to be discovered floating about in a sea of unsubstantiated, unjustified, normative, or prescriptive judgments. If we still want to be normative or prescriptive, very well, but let us not try to defend ourselves logically or scientifically.

But consider another type of example. One of the contemporary generation of better-known American philosophers, Professor William Frankena, is also sometimes regarded as a philosophic analyst. Partly in preparation for this chapter, I have read his essay, "Toward a Philosophy of Moral Education."[2] I find that here is a philosopher who claims that we ought to teach morally but produces no convincing case in behalf of what education is supposed to be moral about. As far as I can detect, Professor Frankena advances little beyond the well-meaning sentiments of old-fashioned country preachers about the good life, except that his own "meanings" are perhaps still hazier. It is as though, since there is "no logical connection" between descriptive and prescriptive judgments anyway, we might as well be as arbitrary and sentimental as we please when we recommend "moral education."

To conclude all that can be said here about philosophic forms of analysis, their contribution has been primarily twofold. On the one hand, they force us to be more precise in our language. Thus, we are cautioned against looseness in all forms of communication. On the other hand, we are admonished against the false dichotomy of the descriptive and prescriptive—a dichotomy that is held to be as chronic in education as in any other human enterprise involving supposed meaning.

Turning to the existentialist, can we learn from him, too? As in the case of the linguistic analyst, only a few impressions are possible here. Nevertheless (as I shall contend later in discussing philosophies of religion and education), the central significance of existentialism, for me at least, is that it has brought us back to where and who we are. Indeed, under the dehumanizing impact of industrialism, technology, and the physical sciences, it is as if we had almost forgotten ourselves. Jean-Paul Sartre, doubtless the most famous of living existentialists; another Frenchman, Nobel Prize winner Albert Camus; Paul Tillich, the late American philosopher of religion; the late Karl Jaspers in Germany; the late Martin Buber, great Jewish philosopher —these twentieth-century thinkers have expressed a similar concern. They are forcing us to swing back to man and his existence, to the core of his nature, his own significance, his sense of poignant self-awareness—if only at the final cost of discovering, paradoxically, his profound meaninglessness.

To be sure, like the logical analyst, the existentialist leaves many of us with feelings of negativity or doubt. For he, too, repudiates much of our intellectual tradition—

certainly much of our Judeo-Christian philosophy and theology. Some existentialists contend that "God is dead," and that the sooner we realize this "truth" the better. Thus, for many of us, Camus and Sartre may be very hard to take. But so too, at times, are the more conciliatory existentialists, such as Tillich.

At the same time, although personal identification of one's own existence is the key to existentialism, it is not so philosophically anarchistic as I may be misleading you to suppose. For example, Jaspers and Buber are also profoundly aware of the importance of other selves. Perhaps a more accurate term, then, is *intersubjectivity*. It is not merely *my* subjectivity that is important; equally important is *yours*. Hence, some existentialists express genuine concern for sociality along with personality.

Do we detect a significance here for education? The viewpoint, broadly expressed, may be nothing new, yet we need to hear it loudly and distinctly. The challenge to the educational leader is to help each person become aware of himself and of his relation to other selves in a more authentic sense than ever before. Related positions, such as existential psychoanalysis and certain forms of Oriental thought, tend to converge here, too: however diverse they are in other respects, intensified awareness is central to all of these positions. Therefore they defy every tendency toward depersonalization as symbolized by teaching gadgetry, by computerized evaluatings, and by other sterile devices of our mechanical age.

By contrast, good education is good only to the degree that it provides face-to-face encounters between children, between teachers and children, and between parents and every other member of the educational community. Here is one statement (written in 1854) by the father of existentialism, Soren Kierkegaard, the Danish philosopher:

. . . to be a teacher does not mean simply to affirm that such a thing is so, or to deliver a lecture. . . . No, to be a teacher in the right sense is to be a learner. Instruction begins when you, the teacher, learn from the learner, put yourself in his place so that you may understand what he understands and in the way he understands it.[3]

Kierkegaard's insight has been elaborated and deepened by contemporary existentialists, especially Buber. The theme is dialogue, Buber's whole viewpoint being epitomized as "dialogic philosophy" in his most famous book, *I and Thou*, and also in *Between Man and Man*.

This is about as far as we can go toward answering our first question: What can educational leaders learn from present-day philosophers of ethics? I have tried to suggest, but only to suggest, that they can learn a good deal from at least two influential viewpoints. Turn then to our next large question: Granted the significance and relevance of both viewpoints, is there no approach more satisfactory, more persuasive and pertinent, than these?

I contend that there is, although the third alternative is neither so academically fashionable nor so precisely developed as one could wish. It even claims no agreed-upon label. But let us call it, very awkwardly, a *psychocultural approach* to the ethical tasks of education. Anticipated at several previous points in the course of this book, this third alternative often supersedes the other two because, for one thing, it is peculiarly interdisciplinary—that is, it is not "pure" or exclusive philosophy in the sense that, say, linguistic analysis sometimes claims to be "pure," nor is it immersed so fully in the depths of "existence" as is existentialism.

Thus our present approach is hardly a neatly contrived theory, if only because it constantly depends upon the human sciences and the arts. Even so, seminal thinkers have been contributing to it. In Europe, for instance, one could mention Max Weber, Émile Durkheim, R. H. Tawney, Harold Laski, and, a little later, Julian Huxley. In America, when we think of psychocultural ethics, we immediately recall diverse scholars of recent generations, such as George Herbert Mead, John Dewey, Ernst Cassirer, Kurt Lewin (the last two, expatriates from Hitler's Germany), Clyde Kluckhohn, and Lawrence K. Frank.

Let us select a few characteristics of the psychocultural viewpoint. In their provocative and far-reaching book *The Social Construction of Reality,* Berger and Luckman emphasize "world-openness" as one basic characteristic. By this term they mean that human beings are open to the course of evolution and life rather than handicapped by alleged "iron laws" of history and nature—a feature of this openness being as reminiscent of the pioneering American philosopher William James as it is of the later eminent social psychologist, Gordon Allport. Man is *Becoming* (the title of Allport's famous book); man is dynamic; man is resilient; man is self-creating.

Another fruitful approach regards man as a participative and associating animal. The venerable notion that man is supremely selfish and aggrandizing (a notion rationalized by "social Darwinism" in behalf of the capitalist, competitive ideology) is no longer considered tenable by any of the scholars I have mentioned, or by numerous others. Like lower animals in general, man in his fundamental nature is much more cooperative than otherwise. This contention may still upset many of us, including young learners, because we have been taught to believe that economics won't work in the long run unless people are engaged in profit-making. Not that self-interest plays no genuine role in human experience. Even more pervasive, nevertheless, is the much larger place, both biologically and culturally, of the social interest of men.

Consider once more the philosopher Mead, who tried to build his whole conception of man around what he called the "self-other process." By this he meant that each self, far from centering in some inner kernel (as the existentialist likes to suggest), is very largely the product of other selves. All of us, if you wish, are constantly role-playing. Thus we gradually develop multiple, sometimes harmonious, images of our personalities in the cultural context of our existence.

In this psychocultural approach, we ought also to include the power of men conceived not only as sharing and participating but as directing and innovating. The central theme is well expressed in *Man Makes Himself*, by the archaeologist V. Gordon Childe. Still more influentially, Julian Huxley portrays—far above the level of nonliving nature, and also above the level of animals and plants—the "postorganic" level of one species only: man. Man alone possesses the capacity to be aware of and to engage in his own deliberate development. The paleontologist and Jesuit philosopher Teilhard de Chardin has sought to complement Huxley by contending that this capacity leads also to human convergence.

Here it is well to reintroduce a favorite term of my own: social-self-realization. By this, please recall, I do not mean merely self-realization or self-actualization but, rather, a more explicit and precise delineation of the fulfillment of the self's dynamic powers interpreted as a continuous, cooperative, social process. Self and society are *reciprocal;* neither is regarded as the sufficient cause of the other.

Social-self-realization can, I have suggested, crystallize as the supreme value of human life. Also, it is supported by an increasing, though far from complete, body of research. (Nor, for that matter, are any other descriptive judgments complete, so long as they are properly subjected to precise analyses of further evidence and further validation.) But social-self-realization, in any case, is much more than a descriptive generalization of the self-other process. That is, if you agree thus far in accepting the value of social-self-realization for your own self and your own circle of other selves, and if you have reason from your own observation and experience to suppose that these other selves incline to accept a similar value, then you can maintain with them, and they with you, that *social-self-realization is not only descriptively but prescriptively demonstrable.*

Of course, the analyst is likely at this point to protest: "You're begging the question! You're jumping from a descriptive to a normative judgment." Even assuming it possible to describe the value of social-self-realization (and no one denies, in view of our still limited knowledge of human behavior, that this is surely difficult enough), the bridge from *is* to *ought,* and thus to ethical justifiability of its acceptance, has by no means been constructed. Suppose we tackle this objection.

The term I must introduce next in our discussion of psychocultural ethics is *consensual validation*—a term by no means original, yet thus far only partially clarified. The practical question it raises is whether educational leaders are compelled either to conclude, as Professor Martin seems to be suggesting, that a logical fissure divides the descriptive and prescriptive spheres of education (in brief, a curriculum of, say, established "evidence" versus a curriculum of "arbitrary" purposes) or to include "moral education" in the schools by resorting, with Professor Frankena, to normative platitudes.

Surely the motivation of consensual validation is to seek ethical justification for what one can believe in and be committed to—a justification left unsubstantiated by philosophic analysts and by existentialists as well. Unless we are willing to settle for the dualism of the former, or for temptation to retreat to the primarily affective subjectivity of the latter (granting again that neither of these viewpoints can ever be encapsulated so simply), we are entitled to some alternative other than either of these.

Consensual validation requires at least four related steps, although not necessarily in consecutive order. The first step is the provision of evidence—maximum evidence of what we desire. By "we" I mean human beings of all races, all religions, all classes, all cultures. The more we can learn and discover from the sciences and arts of man, from the experience and testimony of other people as well as of ourselves, the better. Here the logical analyst could be very helpful by insisting on meaning, on refining our understanding of the evidence of what we actually value. In another way, the existentialist is equally helpful because he keeps reminding us of the necessity to come back to ourselves in order to search into and share our inner feelings, our hopes, and even our dreams. I see no reason why we cannot borrow from both the analyst and the existentialist, insisting upon every conceivable variety of evidence—indeed, we *must* borrow from them.

The second step is maximizing communication. What a giant step this is! Although Marshall McLuhan has made us aware most volubly of the revolution in communication, most of us are only vaguely familiar with its eruptive impact. Yet we cannot hope to achieve consensual validation at all unless we try patiently to communicate our concerns, whatever they may be.

To take a single illustration, suppose that I desire the value of recognition. Of course, I also desire apparently much simpler values, such as nourishment. But, perhaps unlike many of my fellows who obviously desire food, I must confess that, at times, half-consciously, at least, I have received only meagerly the recognition that I value far more than I value food. The result is that sometimes I feel woefully frustrated—for example, when I write books that few people ever read.

But what about those who do not struggle to fulfill the value of recognition in such laborious, deliberate ways? Is this a desire common among them as well? Even though psychocultural evidence is far from complete, it is substantial enough to justify an affirmative answer: the desire for recognition may well prove to be a ubiquitous aspiration of man. The self-other process of Mead is one supportive theory: Is not recognition a social event in the relations of human beings? Buber's dialogue of *I and Thou* is another. And there are still other theories, such as existential psychoanalysis, which, influenced by Freud and now the neo-Freudians, highlights the necessity from infancy onward for the loving concern of parents.

To return, then, to myself, I contend that when the linguistic analyst tries to separate the *description of my desire* for recognition from the *prescription of my desirability*, he is trying to bypass a route that has already been established and confirmed *in my own experience*. I, at least, am therefore aware of the route that I travel from fact to norm. And I am aware, further, that, when denied the satisfaction of moderate recognition, I am unhappy. When I do receive that satisfaction, *I* feel better and happier.

Do *you* know this and feel this way, too? Do *you* hear my question? Let us then convey our experience to each other. Let us also go to authorities and strengthen our awareness with as much of the testimony of experience and research as we are able to command. But not all of this effort need be shared verbally or cognitively. *Listen* at this moment, this silent moment—listen. . . . : Do *we* not in this very gesture seek to become attuned to our affective recognition of each other? And do we not, by virtue of this very communion, find that together we have crossed the chasm between the descriptive and normative spheres of our human experience? For have we not, although perhaps at times more nonsymbolically than otherwise, discovered a common value which we can then proclaim to be desirable to both of us?

In all of this, a term previously mentioned and sometimes heard not only among existentialists but even among some philosophic analysts seems especially appropriate: *intersubjectivity*. In order for any communicating persons, including scientists, to function well, they must begin with their own immediately experienced perceptions and then seek common ground upon which they can share these perceptions.

The preceding comment leads to our third step, which I shall call *maximum agreement*. At some point we have to ask, "Despite the inevitable limitations of evidence as well as of communication—nonverbal as well as verbal, affective as well as cognitive—must we or must we not finally agree on the desirability of recognition as a value?" You may still reply: "Well, I, for one, do not. I am unconvinced that recognition is important to my own prescription of the good life."

Very well, then, let us reconsider this value. We shall have to refine its meaning further with all the assistance we can obtain from linguistic analysts. We shall try, as existentialists, to identify with one another more directly. Sometime or other, nevertheless, we do have to reach agreement, if only to agree upon our (partial or total) lack of agreement thus far. No one is likely to wait forever; particularly in important matters of everyday life one must make decisions. Often, moreover, each of us must make them in conjunction with another person, or several, or even many. Some agreements, to be sure, are more urgent than others; political choices, especially, are only too commonly reached impulsively rather than on the basis of information. Thus we should even develop the habit of encouraging disagreement if thereby we can engage in further exploration of the factors involved and then proceed to stronger, more plausible agreements than before.

The fourth and final step in consensual validation requires only brief comment, since it too has been anticipated. This step involves active testing and retesting of our agreements. To recall Allport and other authorities on psychocultural ethics, the growing, "becoming," evolving nature of man is such that we have to come back again and again in order to review and reappraise the judgments that we have reached. Thus the overarching norm of social-self-realization itself demands constant modifying and revalidating in the light of experiential situations, whether these be in the classroom, the superintendent's office, the community, or our own homes.

Perhaps we are now prepared to underscore our preceding question: Is there an ethical posture for educational leaders that might provide a more satisfying guide than either of the other guides selected for consideration—linguistic analysis and existentialism? I have tried to suggest that, although we may benefit from both positions, a more promising theory is psychocultural ethics.

The significance of this theory, however, requires one additional concept. I shall term it *empirical universalism,* in the hope of tying together many strands. By empirical universalism I am simply pointing toward the consensual validations that are reached through collective experiences. That is, in the light of the best evidence available, in the light of optimal ways of communication, in the light of whatever maximum agreements we may reach, and lastly in the light of the tested modifications that can then take place, we may begin to establish consensual validations ranging all the way from interpersonal and intersocial to intercultural and international universals. Thereby these universals embrace not only the desires of men but their ultimate desirabilities as well.

An admirable book by W. Warren Wagar, *The City of Man,* helps to highlight this contention. Professor Wagar says that the most compulsive of all empirical universals is world community—a planetary conception of ourselves and our most compelling human purposes. Today, with the swift advances in technology, in the behavioral sciences, and in the arts, we are able to discover (and are already discovering) the common human denominators, not only in terms of what values we can accurately describe, but of what we can defensibly prescribe as well. The city of man in this light thus becomes the most urgent of all empirical universals. In our own terms, it emerges directly from the psychocultural approach to ethics. And it is grounded in social-self-realization as both fact and norm.

Our concluding question: What working priorities for educational leaders can be erected upon the ethical foundations laid thus far? Of these priorities, a central one is to channel the process of consensual validation toward continuous, testable operations. I do not, obviously, suggest that such a process is ever perfectly attainable; rather, it becomes a norm by which to measure attainability in varying degrees. Consensual operation means the "self-other process," with all that this connotes. It means the evolutionary "world-openness" of people toward both nature and human nature. It means, in turn, major restructuring of education on all levels and in virtually all countries.

But the truth is that the wider and richer implications of consensual validation are still either largely ignored or, at best, clumsily carried into educational practice. Paternalism, arbitrariness, and hierarchical administrative machinery continue to be dominant. Timeworn habits of learning and teaching, attacked over a century ago by Kierkegaard, still remain much too brittle and sterile.

The needed ethics points, accordingly, to widespread curriculum planning, not only by educational leaders but, above all, by both students and teachers. In terms of consensual validation, both groups are required to take major, active part in all designing and all decision-making in education. More specifically, to select one instance, faculties at every level should be directly involved in screening and selecting new staff. Indeed, school superintendents and other officials should have no authority to appoint teachers at all; rather, they should participate only in advisory roles. Teachers, above all, should have primary responsibilities. But to function effectively they must also learn how to engage meticulously, constantly, and normatively in elaborating and applying *all four crucial steps* of consensual validation.

The scandalous breakdowns that have occurred on campuses and in public-school systems of the United States alone are largely due, I am convinced, to failure to comprehend or to practice one or more of these four steps. Nevertheless, we *are* learning, and learning fast. Changes are occurring on virtually every campus. The rightful roles of students and faculties are gradually being recognized— recognized not so much because university administrations and trustees have miraculously become enlightened, but because they were too unenlightened for too long a time to anticipate what would happen. The Cox report at Columbia is only one signal of the need for new university structures that rest on the kind of modernized ethical base here presupposed throughout.

Nor may we expect that the upsurge of student power in many countries will soon subside. On the contrary, we are beginning to perceive its effect, downward, at precollege levels. A recent news report, for example, tells of 30 or more

Negro high-school students in a small Southern community who were jammed into jail because they dared to express their constitutional rights against discriminating practices. Hazardous as predictions of human behavior often are, I predict that we will hear more and more from secondary students unless traditional administrative policies are speedily updated.

Perhaps by now the impression has emerged that my chief recommendation would be to liquidate the educational leader entirely! By no means. In terms of the ethical conception toward which we have been pointing, he becomes more influential and effective than ever before. The distinction must be drawn, however, between the educational *administrator* and the educational *leader*. Strictly speaking, the competent administrator is one who facilitates and thus skillfully implements policies, but he never properly determines these policies—in our language, he does not himself formulate normative judgments which are then channeled into decisions and practices. The guiding norms of a school system are articulated and sanctioned by all participants—teachers, students, parents, citizens— and then translated into working programs. The administrator's task, meanwhile, is to carry out these policies and programs in classroom activity, in teacher personnel practices, and in a myriad of additional functions.

But the educational leader (although he may sometimes merge his administrative competencies with those of genuine leadership) has an even more crucial role to perform. He is, above all, a person of imagination and audacity. Hence he encourages his community, both outside and inside the school proper, to act upon its own descriptive and prescriptive values as these derive from psychocultural experience. In this difficult and never terminated obligation, he encourages "dissensual" as well as consensual dialogue. Therefore he recognizes the inevitability and even the desirability of conflict. But he also provides opportunities for resolution of conflict by facilitating maximum application of each major step in the total normative process of consensual validation itself.

What, then, are the goals that ought to be achieved and toward which the educational leader ought to serve as leader? One goal, more imperative than all others combined, is probably also the most neglected by American education. This is to join in the construction and implementation of empirical universals—above all, the city of man—and to accomplish this by recreating a curriculum centered both in human problems and in human expectations.

Immediately, a hundred complex but exciting new opportunities occur—many anticipated in previous pages. Without further elaboration, I shall recall merely two of them. One, of course, is the question of national sovereignty by contrast with the norm of world sovereignty. Another is the disturbing threat of uncontrolled population and, commensurately, the huge task of worldwide birth control.

Equally worth reiterating is the need for direct attention to axiological aspects of both the curriculum and the professional preparation of educational personnel. Here, two further ways have been suggested. One is to include moral education in the public schools. By this I certainly do not mean the old-fashioned maxims about proper conduct that used to be termed "character education." To compartmentalize ethics, and to treat it as just another subject, is not a solution; nor is the scheme to weave unobtrusive moral questions through the curriculum. (Watered-down treatments of "moral and spiritual values" are better not included at all.) Pervasive and forthright consideration of ethical problems is what is called for.

A second practical way of aiming at such difficult objectives is to assure professional concentration upon the fundamental questions of ethics that I have tried to exemplify.

This requires not only that they be given a very definite place in teacher education at the preparatory stage but likewise that regularly scheduled, professional in-service workshops be made available to both faculties and leaders.

In an important sense, ethics is the most indispensable of all humanistic disciplines. For it is, or could prove to be, *the* discipline most qualified to encourage leaders—and even more, teachers and students—to search for the most impelling of all solutions to the problems that modern man encounters. Education's obligations therefore prove as broad as its latent capacities to accept these obligations prove powerful. Yet only in close collaboration with other institutions, such as those of politics and religion, can education hope to succeed in the attempt. I offer this plea in the full spirit of consensual validation toward the most supreme of all empirical universals: mankind itself.

Let Wagar speak, then, for all of us:

> Whoever enlists in the cause of man in this age will find no time for nostalgia. We are the link between the traditional civilizations of a well-remembered past and the emergent world civilization. We stand between. If we break under the strain, there will be no future. All posterity is in our keeping. Such a task against such towering odds joins man to man and weaves meaning into the vast fabric of confusion. It can be the difference between the life and death of the soul.[4]

8. Anthropotherapy: Toward Theory and Practice

It was the American philosopher Charles Peirce who first persuasively contended that concepts have the power to remake reality by discharging into meanings that were not hitherto available to some part of man's experience—thus enabling man to reinterpret and often to control that experience so that it no longer means what it meant before.

Every such explosive concept is, of course, the end-product of a long chain of earlier concepts. In the behavioral sciences, as in the physical sciences, no meaning is ever totally new. At times, nevertheless, a concept is invented that manages to crystallize and integrate a number of previously diffuse and sometimes even contradictory meanings into a newly convergent formulation.

Anthropotherapy, I shall argue, could prove to be this kind of concept. I say "*could* prove" for two reasons. First, a good deal of theoretical elaboration is demanded beyond the bare outline to be presented here. Secondly, and surely crucial in terms of the Peircian philosophy of science, the worth of the concept will depend upon prolonged experimental application in a variety of research situations. As an introduction to both obligations, I shall regard my presentation as merely a theoretical prolegomenon.

Although I have been unable to discover in the literature any explicit reference to the term "anthropotherapy," it is anticipated in dozens of important works. "Social psychiatry," which Marvin Opler especially has done so much to promote,[1] is one such anticipation. George Spindler, whose anthropological interest in education overlaps with mine, mentions the term "cultural therapy," although in a narrower sense than I would intend.[2] More widely, many suggestions are to be found in *Human Organization*, the journal of the Society for Applied Anthropology, and occasionally in the *American Anthropologist*. Certainly some of the most important recent theory in both psychiatry and anthropology, as well as in other behavioral sciences, points toward the target of meaning I intend.

If, nevertheless, these contributions provide at best only a direction, an obvious and important reason for this insufficient conceptualization centers in the infancy, or at most the adolescence, of the whole "culture and personality" field. True, the pioneering studies of such anthropologists as Margaret Mead, Ruth Benedict, and Bronislaw Malinowski radiate with psychocultural significance. Yet it is helpful to recall that one of the first invitations ever extended by anthropologists to psychologists to consider possible intermeshings was published under the sponsorship of the Viking Fund some twenty years ago; that Géza Róheim and Edward Sapir, in their very different ways, were just beginning to open the field theoretically in the decade or two preceding this conference; that Ralph Linton and Abram Kardiner formed virtually the first anthropologist-psychiatrist team in the 1940's; that the first extensive collection of writings was published under the editorship of another anthropologist and psychiatrist, Clyde Kluckhohn and Henry A. Murray, as recently as 1953; and that the first textbook on personality and culture was published just a year later, by John J. Honigmann.

The struggles to achieve a mature formulation have been made arduous by other factors than that of extreme youth. For one thing, the majority of specialists in both anthropology and psychology have continued their preoccupations with circumscribed research of orthodox types that have kept them divided oftener than not. More fundamentally, a substantial theoretical literature has opposed any serious rapprochement. For example, Leslie White and his disciples have been militant in their opposition to all efforts to psychologize culture. Nor is it difficult to discover equally strong resistance to the anthropologizing of personality—particularly and painfully noticeable in professional teacher-training institutions. Not only does anthropology remain a largely neglected discipline among these schools, but major stress continues to be placed upon psychologies of education that are conspicuous chiefly for their lack of sophisticated attention to the social and cultural dimensions of human learning and development. The average teacher in the average classroom of the average community in all countries is almost totally illiterate in the field of personality and culture.

Several further reasons may occur as to why we have not hitherto seemed ready for the conception of anthropotherapy, but I shall choose two only. One reason stems from a reluctance in conventional scientific thought to come to grips with the axiological aspects of either psychology or anthropology. This reluctance is not, of course, confined to these two disciplines—it extends to all sciences, physical and behavioral alike. I need not belabor here the reasons that issues of value in science have so frequently been by-passed; they have been considered often. What is important is that these issues have only recently begun to receive the kind of attention that philosophers have always insisted they deserve. This attention, in turn, is of two kinds. To adopt the terminology of Ernest Nagel,[3] a behavioral scientist may make "characterizing value judgments" that simply describe a condition in an animal or a group of people which appears to be diseased or otherwise suffering from some malfunction. But he may also make "appraising value judgments"—that is, judgments leading him to conclude that such a condition is undesirable and in need of curative treatment according to norms that he holds of animal or group health. (Nagel's usage, the reader will have perceived, parallels our own terminology of "descriptive" and "normative," as well as "diagnostic" and "prognostic," judgments.)

The kind of concern with issues of value that has achieved most respectability among behavioral scientists, when they are concerned at all, has been confined chiefly to characterizing rather than to appraising value judgments. Indeed, to a great extent, the knotty questions involved in the latter have not even been adequately clarified. Until they are clarified further, attempts to move from the stage of descriptive or characterizing value judgments about personality and culture to the stage of prescriptive or appraisable value judgments will continue to be restricted.

The other reason that I am able to note here for the tardiness of adequate conceptualization emerges from the conflict and uncertainty that prevail within contemporary social institutions as to their own various and desirable roles in the wider culture. Again I cannot examine here the reasons for this situation; they extend deep and far. The relevant fact is that these institutions are also uncertain, if the possibility occurs to them at all, as to how such disciplines as psychology and anthropology could perform useful collaborative functions that might, in turn, lead to more adequate role performance by the institutions themselves.

Almost any major social institution—political, economic, religious, educational—illustrates my contention. The one with which I happen to be most familiar is as good as any, however. Most thoughtful critics of education will agree that the present period affords a sorry spectacle of cross-purposes, opportunism, vituperative accusations and counter-accusations about almost every phase of school theory and practice.

Yet, with few exceptions, two of the most valuable resources by which this unhappy and dangerous situation could be attacked are oftener than not ignored: the resources of philosophy, and the sciences of man. True, psychology among all the behavioral sciences receives limited attention. Even granting, however, that at times it is studied effectively or that some school psychologists succeed in helping youngsters to cope with their personal troubles, can one discover anywhere a single full-time school anthropologist? The contention that education is the central institutional agency of the reciprocal enculturative processes of transmission and innovation, and that it could function much more successfully were its roles as such an agency clarified and implemented through systematic, testable action research in the human sciences working in close conjunction, is a contention that has not so far as I know been clearly recognized in America or in any other country.

The chronic confusions of education—confusions which, I repeat, are by no means confined to this institution but are typical of most other social institutions—are compounded again by the problem of values. Characterizing value judgments are constantly made concerning education. So, too, are appraising value judgments. In certain respects, accordingly, few educational theorists would deny that the contents and processes of education *are* laden with values, or that they *should* thus be laden. The trouble arises from the fact that neither kind of value judgment is clearly perceived or differentiated in everyday educational experience. Rather, both characterizing and appraising value judgments are usually made haphazardly, impulsively, half-consciously if not unconsciously, and even contradictorily by teachers, administrators, parents, students, and citizens in general. They are made in these ways because no discipline in theory or practice is available by which they might be made in any better way. Education, by and large, is an axiological morass.

At the same time, education assuredly is not to be held wholly responsible for its own ineptitudes. After all, education is peculiarly the creation of culture as a whole—in its most comprehensive sense, the central institution through which every culture perpetuates and modifies the customs, habits, values, and other accretions of human evolution that *are* the stuff of culture. The weaknesses and strengths of any kind of education are inextricably bound to weaknesses and strengths of the wider human milieu. In contemporary American life, for example, its own professionals— the so-called educationists—are seldom taken seriously by other professionals, a fact supported by the relative rarity of anthropologists who are eager to cooperate with educationists in the cultural laboratory of the school itself. If, indeed, it is true that the school is derelict in drawing upon the resources of anthropology to vitalize its own roles, it is equally true that most experts in the field of personality and culture frequently ignore the school as too far removed from their own cherished location in the academic sanctuary.

The principal purpose of the discussion thus far has been to clear the ground. The impression that I hope emerges is that the past forty years have been a period of searching for, rather than achieving, a mature interdisciplinary conception of man-in-culture that is operable throughout institutional experience. The past two decades have been devoted, in greater part, to channeling, reshaping, and unifying the resources germane to this very large task. The progress that has been accomplished is well exemplified by Milton Singer's "Survey of Culture and Personality Theory and Research." That other behavioral sciences besides psychology and anthropology are indispensable to the field is indicated by Singer's inclusion of sociologists and social psychologists. He concludes: "The culture and personality approach thus requires an alternating and almost simultaneous use of two different perspectives—that of culture and that of the individual person." Moreover,

> If personality and culture theory does not depend for its derivation on a unique source of data but consists of a variety of constructions from similar bodies of data, then it is equally true that the validation of the theory does not depend on establishing correspondence with a single body of data.[4]

And just as the data and their validation are multiple, so, too, are the methodologies by which the data are interpreted and applied in action. One of the important virtues of the personality and culture movement is that it is anti-reductionist.

Let me turn now to a set of working propositions which, though by no means undebatable, are essential to the task of conceptual formulation. In stating them, it is necessary to be both selective and abbreviative. They are indebted to many more scholars than it is possible to mention. Nevertheless, I do wish to name those who have especially influenced this quest for convergence.

Among philosophers, John Dewey, George Herbert Mead, Ernst Cassirer, and Alfred North Whitehead will surely occur to you again. Among psychologists we recall Erich Fromm, Lawrence K. Frank, Kurt Lewin, Gardner Murphy, Hadley Cantril, Abraham Maslow, and Harry Stack Sullivan. Among anthropologists, besides those named earlier, I select only Alfred L. Kroeber, A. I. Hallowell, Dorothy Lee, Ashley Montagu, David Bidney, Morris Opler, Florence Kluckhohn, and Laura Thompson. All these scholars, and several I have not mentioned, wonderfully exemplify concerted opposition not only to reductionism but also to any tendency to splinter the image of man. Even more appropriate to this discussion is the fact that they are opposed to the exclusion of axiological considerations and denounce every attempt to rigidify, absolutize, or reify our knowledge of culture.

1. Man and nature, and therefore man and culture, are engaged in *continuous transactions*—complementary sharings of experience—in which each is modified endlessly by the impact of the other. Bifocal vision is the corollary of these transactions.

2. Man, like most other animals, engages in *both conflicting and cooperating experiences* throughout life. On the postorganic level of evolution, however, contrasted with both the preorganic and organic levels, a mutation or series of mutations has occurred which enables *homo sapiens*, its indigenous species, to engage in the control and direction of his conflictive-cooperative life by consciously planned deliberations and actions. This is not to say, of course, that man invariably utilizes this capacity even in small part, or that when he does utilize it he is always successful. Failures are abundant. It is to say that to a degree far beyond that of any other animal, man *has* the capacity, and that oc-

casionally he learns to utilize it quite efficiently. In short, he learns to recognize, to analyze, to reorganize, and to direct both the conflicts and the cooperations in which he is forever involved during the course of his evolution.

3. Conflict and cooperation are important instances—in various respects probably the most important—of values that are as universal to man as evolution. About both of them we constantly make *characterizing value judgments*. These in turn become *appraising value judgments* when we decide that a case of human conflict or human cooperation is desirable or undesirable. When this occurs, some added criterion becomes necessary by means of which to judge the case in one way or the other.

4. The dominant criterion of value by which appraising judgments of such values or disvalues as conflict and cooperation are determined may be expressed by the term *social-self-realization*. Its meaning has been developed in earlier pages, but let us refocus on it here. In essence, it symbolizes both the desire and the desirability of human beings to fulfill themselves individually and collectively to the maximum of their physical-emotional-intellectual powers, and to do so both as single personalities and in relation to other personalities living in many kinds of simple or complex social institutions. Social-self-realization, therefore, is both polaristic and organismic. Empirically, its expression ranges in time and place from strongly personalistic to strongly sociocultural behavior. Yet it is never purely one or the other: no human being is ever wholly self-contained, and no social institution or cultural order is ever devoid of individuals who differ among themselves.

At the same time, social-self-realization is not a universal norm in any absolute sense. All we can claim is that increasing, although still limited, evidence from the sciences of man supports the contention that a very large proportion of our species aspires to its attainment. This is true even though the behavior of some individuals and groups militates against or even denies it, and even though the precise ways in which the aspiration is expressed vary widely both within and between the cultures of the world. In any case, those of us who join in this normative consensus are also joining in one of the most empirically universal of appraising value judgments.

5. While it is unnecessary for all behavioral scientists to guide their investigations by the value of social-self-realization or some symbolic equivalent, it is both necessary and desirable for many behavioral scientists to do so. These are, of course, the scientists who are interested in the *active and practical application* of their knowledge to man's quest for a fuller, richer life on the postorganic evolutionary plane. By the same token, they are scientists eager to attack the frustrations and alienations that impede and block such a life. Finally, they are scientists prepared to join not only with philosophers in axiological investigations that could help to clarify the place of values in personality and culture, but also with practitioners in social institutions—education, for one—who are searching for normative goals commensurate with their obligations to the culture in which they function.

6. The empirical universals of *conflict and cooperation should now be judged in the normative context of social-self-realization.* In short, the appraising value judgments to be drawn from the characterizing value judgments that we make about either of these kinds of behavior depend upon whether they enhance or retard personal and cultural fulfillment. Conflict is a negative value when it blocks development toward that goal and a positive value when it enhances such development. The same alternatives apply to cooperation. This is not to contend that conflict and cooperation are exclusively instrumental values; often the experience of engaging in one or the other produces its own

intrinsic value or disvalue, although always in a continuum of means and ends. The crucial point is that, contrary to familiar usage, conflict is by no means always appraisable as a bad or wrong experience, nor is cooperation always appraisable as something good or right.

Education affords an illustration. On the side of personality, a student who generates some form of conflict either within himself or with a required course of study against which he rebels may simply be searching for a more mature and honest way of expressing his own integrity. Conversely, a teacher who lauds a class because every student "cooperates" with her may mean, in fact, that everyone is passively conforming to her own disciplinary rules. On the side of society, the need for appraising value judgments governed by a normative standard is similar. Conflict between groups —as in a union strike—not only may result in better wages for the workers but may provide enriching experiences in a common cause. Again, conversely, cooperation within a group, although as in the example of union solidarity it does often carry its own positive value, may, as in an army or assembly line, produce the negative value of submission to authority or debilitating monotony. In every case, social-self-realization is the normative measuring stick.

7. Anthropotherapy may now be defined in preliminary fashion as *the theory and practice of descriptive and prescriptive human roles*. It provides analyses particularly of conflictive and cooperative situations and makes characterizing value judgments in the light of such analyses. It provides prognoses of these situations and makes appraising value judgments in the light of such prognoses. It operates within social institutions such as education; accordingly, it regards and utilizes enculturation as the inclusive human process not only for transmitting but also for innovating both personal behavior and cultural patterns.

The prefix "anthropo-" is more connotative of the intended meaning than either "psycho-" or "culturo-": it synchronizes both of these two meanings in the bifocal meaning of "man" as personality and culture in continuous transactional relationships.

8. The theory and practice of *psychotherapy* has much to contribute to the development of anthropotherapy. Particularly in neo-Freudian interpersonal psychiatry, one notes not only more and more sensitivity to the sociocultural and ecological matrix, but also more and more explication of the normative character of this applied science. The patient is encouraged to explore without coercion the roots of his own unconscious neurotic or psychotic troubles, but not without consciousness on the part of the therapist as to how they are neurotic or psychotic—that is, destructive—when gauged by the constructive criterion of personal-cultural fulfillment. Unlike some styles of earlier psychotherapy that tried quite unsuccessfully to rule out appraising value judgments, the styles to which I refer by no means rule them out.

Nor do they tend to assume, as did some earlier styles, that conflict is to be judged invariably as disvaluable and cooperation invariably as valuable. Once more, the converse view may lead to a correct diagnosis of the troubles of a patient: he may, for example, fear engaging in any kind of conflict—with an employer, say—and therefore compensate for his fear by a kind of acquiescent cooperation that only drives his misery deeper. In many instances, therefore, "maladjustment" may prove, paradoxically, to be far more desirable as a therapeutic goal than the more comfortable one of "adjustment."

To take education again as an example, any competent school psychologist or counselor is committed, first of all, to performing the role that Fromm calls the "observant participant." He is the kind of psychotherapist who is "fully engaged with the patient" (student), who is "soaked with him, as it were, in this center-to-center relatedness."⁵ A genuine transaction occurs between the two because both patient and counselor are changed by that kind of relatedness. Indeed, what is true of the school counselor extends ideally to every teacher—a term, incidentally, that Fromm himself applies to the effective analyst. And is this not understandable? The destructive and constructive conflicts and cooperations endemic to our age are matters both of acute anxiety and of great potential benefit not only to children so ill as to need psychotherapy; they are now common to a larger and larger proportion of the human race. Certainly they are familiar to young people growing up in our kind of world—a world fraught with dread of thermonuclear annihilation, with political, economic, esthetic, and scientific revolutions, and above all with rapid deterioration of the kinds of moral anchorage provided by traditional customs and religions. In the sense of the term that I am inferring, the thoroughly effective teacher *is* a psychotherapist.

9. In another sense, however, psychotherapy remains much too constrictive a term, too loaded with dubious assumptions which tempt us to believe that virtually all we need in order to cure the ailments of our time is to attack them, as it were, from the inside out, as though the objective world will become healthy and sound only when the subjective psyche has first become healthy and sound. This is the supreme psychotherapeutic fallacy. It is peculiarly dangerous in education because it offers moral sanction for aloofness from the most controversial issues of society and politics. Its bias is correctable only through *the unity of a discipline in which psychotherapy's own theory and practice are amalgamated with the theory and practice of planned sociocultural diagnosis and prognosis.*

Probably the single most essential operating principle that has thus far emerged from the social sciences of planned change is correlative with Fromm's concept of observant participation in psychotherapy. To be effective in the long run, planned change cannot be manipulative or superimposed; rather, it requires genuine, pervasive involvement on the part of the applied social scientist in the affective-cognitive experiences of every community where conflict and/or cooperation may have generated any kind of problem in need of resolution. Here the cultural anthropologist contributes most to the required working principle; he has long known that the field experiences of participant observation are indispensable to fruitful results. Even so, the task of bringing about systematized change in any kind of community pattern is arduous indeed—no doubt even more arduous than bringing about change in the personality structure of an individual through psychotherapy. On this score, the hard-headed realism of deterministic anthropology is salutary: to bring about change in human beings, individually *or* socially, is never easy, and sometimes it is apparently impossible.

Nevertheless, with Bidney, I contend that the inference of some anthropologists that culture is the sufficient cause of human change is to commit the "culturalistic fallacy"[6]— the counterpart of the psychotherapeutic fallacy, at the other extreme. Planned improvement of human life could become much less difficult and much more improbable if, by means of the theory and practice of anthropotherapy, we came to accept not only the research axiom of sustained involvement in the life of any culture where personal and social change is contemplated, but the axiological principle that such change must be governed by empirically defensible human goals. Fromm's words apply here at least equally as well to anthropotherapy as to psychotherapy: the "therapeutic aim cannot be achieved as long as it remains limited and does not become part of a wider, humanistic frame of reference"[7]—a frame of reference through which, in the language of this chapter, social-self-realization is globally extended.

10. I conclude this theoretical outline with several major precautionary propositions. The first is that *the axiological unity of mankind has by no means been so well demonstrated as the axiological diversity of mankind.* Florence Kluckhohn's work in variations among value orientations cannot be appreciated too much as a safeguard against oversimplifications about the common denominators among cultural values. In radically different terms, May and Abraham Edel urge a rapprochement between anthropology and axiological theory that again stresses the difficulties, but by no means impossibility, of moving from pluralistic, descriptive comparisons of cultural values to inclusive, normative generalizations about them.

If we regard social-self-realization as this kind of normative generalization, let us note the following precautions that follow from it. The universal significance of social-self-realization has not yet been completely grasped and probably never will be. It is itself subject to refinement in the light of knowledge that we do not yet possess. No two cultures can be expected to understand or explicate its meaning in identical terms. Many cultures are not even prepared to admit that they could benefit by experimentation in behalf of that meaning. Finally, and perhaps most importantly, the distinction between characterizing value judgments based upon descriptive evidence and appraising value judgments resulting in prescriptive programs for testing should always be kept clear.

11. The second precautionary judgment relates to the first. Anthropotherapists engaged in action research must ever be on the alert to accept unanticipated contingencies. Certainly *the methodology of participant observation will at all times encourage every personality and group involved to express fully their own values and other interests accord-*

ing to their own perceptions and not according to the anthropotherapist's. If cultural change then results in some expression of the encompassing normative goal, it occurs because the largest possible proportion of those directly involved wish it to occur. The supreme test of the anthropotherapist's own hypotheses concerning, for example, a destructive intracultural conflict is whether in the behavior of those involved it reduces the anxieties, prejudices, or other disvalues characterizing that conflict and thereby achieves greater justification for the appraising value judgment of social-self-realization than prevailed before.

12. The third precautionary proposition is that *anthropotherapy is not merely the science but the art of planned human evolution.* I do not mean this merely in the trite sense that human behavior, individually or socially, can rarely be reduced to a mathematical equation. Nor do I mean it in the sense only that (as in the case of psychotherapy) feeling, intuition, insight—above all, the unconscious—are critically important. Both of these senses are germane, but I would add a third. Anthropotherapy is an art because it is an experience in the *re-creation* of personality and culture. Just as the psychotherapist can be compared with an artist whose canvas is the patient, so the anthropotherapist, in another sense, is one who aims to reshape not merely personalities as the efficient cause of culture but cultures themselves. The pragmatic test again is relevant: to the extent that a community discovers, for example, the unconscious sources of particular negative values and then proceeds therapeutically to change itself enculturatively in the direction of positive values—to that extent has the community performed a work of re-creation upon and with itself. It has, as it were, drawn closer to its own "ideal superego."

13. As a last precautionary proposition, anthropotherapy, as and if it proves to be the kind of crystallizing concept I

anticipate, requires precise and manifold testing in the clinical laboratories of real communities. The point I wish to underscore, however, is not merely this necessity but also that of *extending limited clinical experience to the wider problems of mankind as a whole*. Microcosmic studies should be extended both across particular cultures and toward a macrocosmic vision of man and his encompassing goals. As Laura Thompson has put it:

> A unified science of mankind is emerging . . . on the basis of new perspectives . . . in the life sciences. . . . Such a science [of mankind] could not be born until social scientists, seeking solutions to urgent human problems, began to question anachronistic models and to alter their working hypotheses in keeping with the conceptual revolution.[8]

Anthropotherapy, I contend, is clairvoyant of this revolution.

9. A Pilot Project for Sex Education

An affirmative, constructive, and creative expression of sexuality is indigenous to the wellbeing of man. It is in terms of this value orientation, which has pervaded the preceding chapters, that ethical education in sexual behavior and attitudes should be undertaken in the schools.

In large part, nevertheless, such an approach is evaded or, at most, verbalized in clichés. A negativistic approach stemming from long religio-cultural traditions and permeated with guilt feelings is far more common in the meta-cultural assumptions that continue to govern much of our education. One result is that many schools of America help to perpetuate the negativistic approach mainly by default —that is, by ignoring the dimension of sexuality, especially in its moral aspects, and thus allowing the inherited orientation, with its dualisms and anxiety-breeding habits, to sicken the lives of uncounted children until they become even sicker adults.

By contrast, a life-affirming psychocultural ethic leads to a number of guidelines as principles that govern effective sex education. Because these are germane to the concrete proposal presented below, it may be helpful to summarize them as succinctly as possible, even though each in itself could receive prolonged consideration:

1. Sexuality is lifelong in its relevance, from birth to death.
2. Sexuality is both descriptive and prescriptive—both what it *is* and what it *ought to be*.
3. Sexuality embraces not merely biology but all the sciences of human behavior, and also the humanities.
4. Teachers require far more competent professional acquaintance with sexuality in all its aspects than they usually receive.
5. Parental support for and involvement in sex education is imperative.
6. Levels of maturation must be considered in dealing effectively with sexual problems.
7. These problems should be introduced into the curriculum by means of systematic, planned study, as well as through "indirect" consideration in various fields not always concerned with them "directly."
8. No aspect of sexuality should be omitted from the curriculum, but aspects selected for consideration should increase in sophistication and technicality with the growing maturity of the pupils.

Many ways of introducing sex education into the curriculum have been suggested by experts (especially commendable are Dr. Mary S. Calderone and the Sex Information and Education Council of the United States), but most efforts thus far have been overcautious. The remainder of this chapter focuses upon only one way rather than diffusing the problem still further. This way—a pilot project—is, I believe, practical for experimentally minded schools. Pilot projects have the virtue of small-scale involvement, so that failure is not so serious as it would be in a school system that had adopted a total plan of curriculum innovation. If the projects succeed, improvements can be effected and the program expanded with more assurance and support. Sex education is very much in need of such innovative, carefully planned pilot projects.

The proposal centers in primary utilization of one division of the behavioral sciences—psychotherapy. Although psychotherapy has hardly achieved full stature as an applied science, most informed educators would agree that it has grown much more rapidly in both theory and practice than is apparent in the programs of American schools. One can think of few areas of knowledge about human beings that are so completely neglected by the typical curriculum. Only on the college level is psychotherapy (or its allied disciplines, psychiatry and psychoanalysis) given any concerted attention, but even on this level it is doubtful whether the average undergraduate receives more than a smattering of understanding of the area when he pursues usual courses in general psychology.

I do not, however, propose as a major pilot project the introduction of a unit of study on the elementary principles of psychotherapy. Although such a unit could prove an interesting experience for, say, seventeen-year-olds, and could be developed by skillful teachers so as to prove both understandable and fascinating, my primary focus here is on a more indirect approach in accordance with principle #7 above—indirect, that is to say, in the sense that psychotherapy as an applied science comes to be learned by experience in therapeutic situations; indirect, also, in that problems of sexuality emerge naturally in the course of such experience rather than by means of superimposition or artificiality.

Before I spell out this proposal, a word should be said about the nature of psychotherapy itself. Let us not try to identify it with the position of any single practitioner or theoretician, whether he be Freud, Sullivan, Rogers, May, or Fromm. Were I more competent in the field, perhaps I should be less easily satisfied with an eclectic position, particularly since I am skeptical of eclecticism in educational philosophy. At the same time, psychotherapy is so very young a discipline that even its own most able exponents are far from agreed in theory. And since they are even less agreed about its possible contributions to educational theory and practice (many psychotherapists have scarcely considered these at all), the most practical course is not to formulate a pilot project in terms of one position but rather to draw upon various resources in terms of their applicability to available educational situations.

But one point at least differs in marked degree from several conspicuous positions. The dominant purpose of attempting a psychotherapeutic approach to sex education is frankly *not* merely that of objective, scientific observation. It is the purpose of deriving from this approach a more solidly grounded, unsentimental, workable series of solutions to problems that are fundamentally ethical in character. In this respect, the proposal is consistent with the object of those advanced in preceding pages—to build a defensible ethical education upon a scientific base. That logical difficulties arise from any such attempt is readily admitted. To dismiss it because of such difficulties is, however, much too easy a way out. The need is not for dismissal, but for frank, discerning assessment of the tasks involved in building a modern ethics, chiefly from the resources of all the human sciences.

Psychotherapy, as I mean the term, is thus an applied science of human behavior devoted primarily to helping a person to discover the nature of himself and his relations to other personalities, as well as in terms of the cultural patterns most important to his own nature, to his development, and to his optimal capacities. "Therapy" is also regarded in a broader sense than is conventional: it connotes the existence of illness or disease which its processes aim to cure, but it likewise embraces the search of the personality, normal or abnormal, for greater and more accurate self- and social awareness. Especially in some of its unused educational potentialities, psychotherapy could prove to be an extraordinarily fruitful process of learning and teaching that interfuses the entire curriculum from the earliest to the latest years of education. In this sense, an "indirect" approach is entirely legitimate.

This pilot project involves five groups of educational participants—members of the administrative staff, a teacher group, a parent group, a high-school student group, and an elementary student group. If resources permit, the first three of these groups could participate initially at about the same time and continue into the period when the last two groups are also active.

1. *The administrative group.* This group, consisting of one or more principals, supervisors, curriculum directors, and counseling officers, understands that the guiding objective is to introduce psychotherapeutic principles into learning experiences of elementary and secondary students, and that one effect of such experiences may be increased competence in dealing with sexual problems. Stated more formally, the project tests both a general and a specific hypothesis—namely, that (a) psychotherapy is a resource of great potential importance to the "health" of personality development; and (b) it can enable the young person to

cope more positively and creatively than hitherto with the ethical aspects of his own sexuality.

The administrative group does not try to test either hypothesis. What it does is to engage briefly, under the guidance of at least one group psychotherapist, in the methods of intragroup relations that can sensitize participants to some of the characteristic roles, tensions, conflicts, withdrawals, manipulations, and similar phenomena that often appear as participants begin to reduce their inhibitions and reveal their feelings. Whether the group decides to continue beyond this brief exposure of, say, three or four sessions depends upon variables that can hardly be considered here. In any case, assuming that they have already endorsed the over-all proposal, this group aims to acquaint itself with the nature of psychotherapy in the broad sense indicated. This is important if only because the field is as yet strange to most educators. A more practical reason, of course, is to enlist the administration's support from their own experience. But it is possible that another byproduct may be eagerness on the part of the group to continue its own involvement simultaneously with that of the parent and teacher groups, to which we next turn.

2. *The parent group.* In accordance with principle #5, parents are also much more likely to support a pilot project if they are clear about its methods and objectives—certainly so in the case of a project as venturesome as the one here proposed. As for the administrative group, it is essential to provide skilled direction—in this case, a group psychotherapist interested in education.

One or both of two forms of parent groups could be organized. The easier group to establish would be made up of fairly typical school-minded parents interested in new ways to learn; therefore they would be considered "normal," as would their children (at least as revealed by school profiles). The other group would be selected because their children suffer from emotional problems about which the parents themselves are troubled. A psychotherapist should attend both groups, which would meet at least once a week in the evening. This experience should continue for some three months and, as in the case of the administrative and teacher groups, should precede the initiation of the student groups for perhaps half of this period.

3. *The teacher group.* Granted that it is possible that the pilot project could be attempted without involvement by either of the groups thus far described (although the proj ect would be strengthened if they were involved), it is impossible to dispense with the teacher group. This necessity is noted in principle #4 above. Moreover, it is possible to provide two groups of teachers, one representing the elementary level, the other the secondary level. The guidance of a psychotherapist is equally essential for both groups.

Teachers should be selected very carefully in terms of their interest in the project, their concern with personality development, their sophistication with regard to sexual problems, and their background in the behavioral sciences. Some previous knowledge of psychotherapy or its allied areas could be an important criterion of selection. Their in-service training for the project should likewise occupy about three months or more of group psychotherapy on a schedule at least as intensive as that of the parent group, in addition to systematic study of the principal theories of psychotherapy and current approaches to sex education. Since so intensive a program could not be carried on effectively while teachers were restricted to regular school schedules, they should have lessened teaching loads or summer workshops offering graduate credit or both. Some participating teachers should be married, with children.

A substantial block of the teacher-preparation period should be devoted to planning the two student-group experiences. At the same time, such preparation should not be overstructured, since both student projects should allow room for flexibility.

As in the case of the parent group, the course of involvement under skilled leadership leads to increasingly explicit attention to the sexual dimensions of personality development and of the relations between these dimensions and those of cultural experience. Since all three adult groups understand the objectives of the project, there is nothing manipulative about such increasing involvement. For this reason, too, increasing attention may well be given to the ethical context of psychotherapeutic experience.

Here, therefore, the professional consultant is urged to recognize that his role is not merely that of an applied scientist but that of an educator familiar with, and to a considerable degree committed to, the value orientation epitomized at the outset. In short, the normative aspect of all three of the group experiences thus far proposed is never suppressed, even when it is not always central to group attention. In earlier terminology, the aim of the pilot project is to enable its participants—particularly the young people who constitute our fourth and fifth groups—to achieve the fullest possible social-self-realization, in which sexual expression is an integral and primary value.

4. *High-school student group.* If enough teachers from the training group are available, it is recommended that four groups of secondary students be selected—two on the senior level (ages 17 and 18) and two on the junior level (ages 14 and 15). One group in each age category should be made up of children with recognized emotional problems. But if only one group is practicable at the outset, it should consist of older, more or less average, "normal" young men and women. In any case, the psychotherapists who have functioned with the adult groups should keep constant tab on the student groups as well.

The high-school group is not necessarily informed at the outset that the twofold purpose of the project is to test the effectiveness of psychotherapy as a learning experience, with special concern for the ethics of sexuality. Such a statement, in any case, carries so little explicit meaning that it could easily set up obstacles to participation. This group would, however, be informed that it is to engage in a novel experience—that of careful discussion of intrapersonal, interpersonal, and personal-cultural problems, in which moral and hence sexual problems are bound to arise.

Since, moreover, the process of learning is permissive (in Carl Rogers' term, client-centered), no agenda is set up and no definite outcome is predetermined. How interesting and fruitful the experience proves to be depends upon the participants themselves. Students also learn that the teachers chosen as resource persons have received special training in this kind of group experience and are always ready to share reactions with their students. The aim of the project, then, is characterized as a quest for deeper self- and social awareness, particularly with regard to problems that generate alternative ways of resolution.

As the project moves forward, the directing teachers introduce concepts from psychotherapy where and when these prove clarifying. For example, since the high-school project is an adventure in group psychotherapy (though not so labeled at the beginning), some of Freud's simpler concepts are gradually introduced—not in a didactic sense but as useful tools of analysis and prognosis. Such familiar terms as id, ego, superego, cathexis, libido, narcissism, and suppression are quite understandable. Some of the concepts of existential psychology and interpersonal psychiatry are also meaningful.

In accordance with principle #8, it is anticipated that during the months of regular sessions (two or three a week, at least), the secondary group will deal with increasingly sensitive topics as these emerge from their participation. Among these topics are the phenomenon of homosexuality, birth-control practices, and erotic patterns before, during, and after marriage. Descriptive resources from anthropology, for example, are useful at this stage, providing cross-cultural perspective. Literature and other arts are also used. Resource persons from various areas of the curriculum as well as from the community (artists, social workers, leaders of youth organizations) should be drawn into the project to place the problems under consideration in familiar cultural contexts. Principle #3 thus becomes more and more operable as ethical aspects of personality development come to the fore. Simultaneously, Freudian concepts are supplemented by functional application of the cultural psychiatry of such authorities as Harry Stack Sullivan.

What, then, began as group psychotherapy in a somewhat restricted sense gradually widens to include both experiential resources and the range of psychotherapeutic concepts. In the same way, ethics becomes increasingly explicit as problems focus upon conflict-choices, such as those which so frequently confront young adults in the relations of the sexes. Careful, inductive consideration of moral options, and of the consequences that alternate choices entail, is imperative. The central role of the teacher here becomes one of moral catalyst, not of moral judge.

Eventually, the principle of consensual validation, discussed in Chapter 7, is introduced as a way of reaching beyond merely individualistic value judgments. While every student participant understands that he is free to dissent or to remain undecided about any issue that has been discussed, the aim should also be expressed of achieving whatever agreement can freely arise from the process. An ethical implication here is that moral questions, especially those involving sexual behavior, are rarely if ever purely personal: obligation and responsibility must be given consideration in the weighing of all options. There is also an epistemological implication: ethical judgments derive from, even though they are not identical with, reliable evidence—evidence which, certainly in the case of human problems, is relational and social as well as particular and individual. Indeed, to complete the philosophic triumvirate, this contribution is ontological as well: for example, all ethical problems, and surely the sexual, are in some ways profoundly existential. Consensual validation requires the interdependence of all three philosophic principles—the axiological, epistemological, and ontological.

5. *The elementary group.* Guideline #1 underscores the lifelong fact of sexuality. Therefore the elementary level is by no means too early to introduce some aspects of the kinds of learning already discussed as appropriate to administrators, teachers, and high-school students. As an integral feature of the proposed project, however, a more indirect approach is appropriate for this group. Certainly at the outset, typical groups of children would not seem feasible for group psychotherapeutic experiences. Moreover, in accordance with principle #6, the kinds of sexual problems that are often crucial to high-school seniors may be neither meaningful nor relevant to children of five or ten years of age. The so-called latency period of pre-adolescent growth provides different intensities of interest than in later periods.

Nevertheless, many of the problems faced by young adults are rooted in infancy and early childhood—an axiom which Freud and his daughter, Anna Freud, perhaps as much as any scientists of human behavior, have established once and for all. One of the most challenging features of this pilot project, accordingly, is to consider how psychotherapy might be introduced into elementary learning and teaching. It is hoped that several of the teachers who have experienced the in-service program described above will undertake to test their leadership skills as early as the nursery school, and from there on up to the secondary level.

I am indebted here to Professor Richard Jones, whose experimental work has led him to conclude that psycho-therapeutic concepts can be fruitfully utilized in conjunction with a variety of learnings appropriate for elementary schools. His use of one such concept is particularly impressive: the stimulation and encouragement of free association (a basic Freudian principle) by the sharing of dreams. Children are often fascinated by their dreams and, with a little encouragement, can be prevailed upon to describe them in classroom situations when they bear upon a learning activity in, say, drawing or clay-modelling, music or dance, reading or social studies. The habit of remembering and sharing can be cultivated by the skillful teacher in much the same way that other habits are cultivated. In this way, Jones believes, children can begin very early to discover some of their own unconscious primary processes. Thereby they are engaging in a simple form of self-analysis which, in turn, could lead to greater self-awareness on conscious and more mature levels.

Obviously, it is by no means easy to encourage dream reportage without forcing or artificiality. One of Jones's suggestions is that the teacher share his own dreams with his students, invite discussion of them, and thereby encourage others to do likewise. Another suggestion is that children be encouraged to share not only their "nightdreams" but their "daydreams" as well, again as relevantly as possible to the learning pattern of the moment. One way to bring about this kind of sharing is to provide periods of silence in which children would be encouraged, not just to "relax" in a routine way, but to fantasize as freely as possible as part of some activity germane to their learning at the time.

Presupposing the kind of teachers selected for this pilot

project, it may be redundant to stress one precaution. However self-confident in their knowledge of psychotherapy, it should not be their prerogative to diagnose emotional disturbances, sexual or otherwise, in the light of dream reportage or of any other data. At most, they may wish to inform professional psychotherapists of any observations that strike them as possibly helpful to such diagnoses. The purpose of dream reportage, for example, is not so much to interpret child behavior as to encourage free association. Only thus far is this purpose properly described as psychotherapy in the narrow sense. But in the broad sense here assumed, it offers striking opportunity to break new ground in learning conducive to personality development.

This chapter, like others, raises a large number of questions that can be answered only by actual attempts on the part of school systems to try out chief features of the proposal. I question whether it would ever be possible to meet all objections in advance. What is needed is the kind of educational imagination that is willing to venture, to profit by mistakes, and to improve by experimentation.

I likewise question whether any of the perplexing issues confronting educators who earnestly wish to come to grips with the ethics of sexuality will be resolved by piecemeal advice on how to tackle the urgent problems raised by young people. A far more promising way is by functional utilization of the emerging sciences of man—sciences which to an appalling extent are still neglected by our schools. Among these sciences, psychotherapy is one of the most exciting and most promising. When it is related, as I have proposed, with continuous concern for genuine moral and cultural issues, sex education should become integral with all creative education.

Part III
Religion and Education
in a Time of Trouble

10. The Restless Alliance

With all the differences that may occur to us when we think of education and religion, they also share much in common. Both are universal to cultural experience. Both are bridges through which man endeavors to relate himself to reality. Both are expressed in symbolic forms. Both have achieved institutional embodiment. Both embrace a bewildering array of habits, practices, rituals. Both are saturated with values. Both involve conceptions of truth. Both have intricate relations to other great human achievements, such as politics, art, science, and philosophy.

It is the relation of education and religion to the last in this list of human achievements— philosophy—that is our central concern here. More precisely, I shall here inquire into the possible significance that religion may have for education when it is reconsidered in the light of contemporary events and contemporary thought.

In common with many other students of the twentieth century, I contend that ours is an age of upheaval—upheaval not only in the political and economic spheres, where, to be sure, overt violence and even the threat of annihilation are most dreadful, but also in every other sphere of man's existence—in morality, in esthetics, in human relations, and, therefore, in education and religion as well.

I shall not try further to document this well-established generalization. Rather, I shall attempt to describe a new rapprochement between education and religion that could, in crucial ways, serve as both catalyst and therapist to both institutions. I do not pretend to know whether the proposal for such rapprochement will be taken seriously enough or widely enough to retard catastrophe, much less prevent it. Yet, unless it occurs, humanity has very little to expect, not only from education and religion, but from other dimensions of life, such as the political. I ask only that my thesis be seriously weighed so that, if it is persuasive, fuller consideration and subsequent action can follow with minimum delay.

Among the many reasons not to be sanguine is the fact that the philosophy of education is not taken very seriously by other intellectual disciplines. Even among philosophers, every other recognized subdivision of the field—such as the philosophy of science or of art—receives far more respectful attention in conferences and in journals. Despite the example of John Dewey, who once defined philosophy as the general theory of education, despite also the concern of some of the greatest thinkers of history, from Plato to John Locke to A. N. Whitehead, the majority of present-day academic philosophers offer little but commonplaces about the educational enterprise.

Whether the same disregard is to be found among scholars in the field of religion I am not in a fair position to say. That they pay some critical attention to education is obvious. But my impression is that, except for concern with particular issues such as church-and-state, or with problems of effective instruction within religious institutions, relatively little serious thought has been expended in recent years on the more urgent and elusive questions that arise when we begin to consider the similar and dissimilar characteristics of education and religion in their comprehensive meanings.

Causes of this dichotomy are several. One probably is that religionists, no less than philosophers and other scholars, are typically so preoccupied with their own specializations that they simply lack the time and interest to pursue interrelationships. Still another explanation must be that since religion and education are now widely regarded in our culture as separate institutions, it is best for the sake of public harmony to keep them as separate as possible. Thus, whatever educational responsibilities religion still retains are best confined, we are told, within its own boundaries— a position maintained by many spokesmen for both institutions. The significance of such common characteristics as I have already noted is rarely examined with care either by religionists or by educationists.

Among philosophers of education the preceding statement must be sharply qualified. Never in the history of American or European education have they agreed on the question of relationship between these great fields. In America, for example, one finds at least two influential philosophic theories that continue to regard all education as essentially religious in character—the Thomist or neo-Thomist, and the objective-idealist. The two theories differ sharply, of course, in some of their underlying philosophic and religious principles—and these differences, in turn, are reflected in differing educational policies and practices.

Thomists, most of whom are affiliated with the Roman Catholic Church, are critical of public education precisely because it excludes indoctrination of their own allegedly infallible beliefs. Objective idealists, most of whom are associated with various Protestant denominations, are obviously not critical on the same ground as Thomists. Nevertheless, they too believe that public education should be permeated with some version of their own idealistic (or sometimes classical-realist) conception of the universe and of man. In at least one respect, therefore, they join hands with the Thomists: any kind of education based on principles devoid of religion, itself conceived by both philosophies of education in the historic terms of some form of transcendental, extranatural, or nonempirical ontology, is an education unworthy of approval and support.

Accordingly, both Thomists and idealists tend to oppose the secularization of educational institutions. And both thereby reveal their ties to a common religious tradition, stemming back far beyond the Middle Ages and extending forward far beyond the Colonial establishment of schools in America.

This tradition, although still powerful in educational theory and practice, has been forced into a defensive position, at least until very recently, by the secularizing pressures of American cultural history. To review these forces here would oversimplify still further. In the context of educational philosophy, however, the single most potent influence against both idealism and Thomism in their educational expressions is fairly easy to distinguish. I refer, of course, to the pragmatic movement of Charles Peirce, William James, and John Dewey, and especially to Dewey's prodigious influence, from his ten-year stay at the University of Chicago at the turn of the century to his death in 1952 and beyond.

To be sure, relatively few of the countless teachers exposed to his ideas in more or less distorted form were given an opportunity to grasp their shattering import. Most teachers, for example, have never recognized that Dewey challenged the foundations of the very religious doctrines that they continued to support in their local church affiliations. Nevertheless, they did absorb into their thinking and classroom activities something of Dewey's view of life and education. Such widely read books as *How We Think* were as firm in their implicit opposition to any kind of authoritarianism, religious or otherwise, as they were supportive of a kind of learning and thinking that places squarely upon man himself the responsibility to direct his own career through his own intelligent powers.

Thus the philosophy of education that was far more widely studied than any other for something like a half century, in the United States and several other countries, provided a completely naturalistic, this-worldly basis for the public schools. The central theme of this philosophy is that human beings can master nature, including their own nature, by putting into thorough and consistent practice the methodologies of experimental science. Education is the primary instrument through which these methodologies can be translated into practical, living experience. The classroom, regardless of its subject matters, is thereby conceived as a laboratory in which children gradually grow into citizens who deal with every aspect of their world (moral, aesthetic, and social as well as physical and biological) reflectively, critically, actively.

The atmosphere permeating this kind of classroom, moreover, is inescapably democratic. For democracy, as Dewey always conceived it, is that way of life in which people of all classes, races, and nationalities are free to engage in the solution of their problems by full and open searching, inventing, sharing, testing.

That the influence of this outlook remains strong both

in professional teacher education and in some segments of the public schools—notably on the elementary level—is indisputable. Equally indisputable, however, is the fact that during the last stage of Dewey's life, and at an accelerated tempo during the years since his death, the philosophy of education that he and his followers propounded has shifted ground. The defensive position which it forced upon the older classical philosophies has now, in one sense, become its own position. Instead of concentrating upon the weaknesses it found in these philosophies, its allies much oftener than not have been compelled to correct misrepresentations and to muster evidence of the superiority of learning and teaching based upon Dewey's theory. The loudest and most influential voices in educational debate are no longer those of the experimentalists-pragmatists but those of its opponents, including traditional religionists.

How can we account for this swing of the pendulum? Not, I believe, by the absurd scapegoating of so-called progressive education. Nor do I believe that conservative critics such as Arthur Bestor, Hyman Rickover, or even James Bryant Conant deserve more than passing comment; superficial and transitory, their voices soon fade. As anyone knows who is moderately familiar with teaching and learning, methods typical of public schools are rarely "progressive" in the pervasive sense that Dewey intended. Although it remains true that many teachers have been influenced by his theory sufficiently to incorporate something of it into their classroom processes, it is even more true that only a few of them have believed or acted consistently in terms of its encompassing experimental meaning. And even if they have wanted to do so, the resistance of communities has often militated against them.

It is on a different level of interpretation, then, that we must seek explanation for the fact that the cultural and educational outlook emerging from the philosophy of pragmatism-experimentalism is considerably less attractive to the present generation than it was in the heyday of its influence. This explanation centers in the adequacy or inadequacy of Dewey's view of man and nature. To put it another way, what disturbs many of his critics (perhaps unconsciously oftener than consciously) is not so much the quality of student performance or classroom standards as it is the permeating implications of such a world view for our age. On this level, and only on this level, can we begin to discover and assess the deeper reasons, not only for the counterattack upon Dewey's educational views, but for the state of confusion in contemporary education as a whole.

If we return, for example, to the major religiously oriented philosophies of education in America, are we not perhaps in a better position to perceive why they have again assumed an aggressive tack? Whether Thomists or idealists of varying expression, they agree that the Dewey world view is wanting because it lacks a final, transcendent referent—some antecedently postulated criterion of truth and value and faith to which all men may turn for indubitable guidance. To say, with Dewey, that man is his own best referent is to say that humanity is its own sufficient guide—a position that they find repugnant. The "quest for certainty" of which Dewey wrote is, for his opponents, a futile quest so long as it relies exclusively on human power and ability. And because the mores of American culture have never reflected, in any case, a consistently naturalistic ethos they are quick to benefit by the cautious retreat from experimental education—a retreat which an age such as ours invites.

By no means, of course, are idealism and Thomism alone in finding fresh opportunity and encouragement to advance their own philosophies of education. Although both of these doctrines may be experiencing something of a resurgence, other directions in educational theory likewise reflect, directly or indirectly, the mood of our time of trouble. We have earlier noted that recent philosophic developments, such as philosophic analysis and existentialism, are attracting able young scholars in education. Linguistic analysts, while sympathetic with the scientific orientation of pragmatism, are critical of its value theory on the ground that its language is imprecise and many of its ethical judgments are unwarranted. Existentialists sometimes find affinity with the religious interests of idealism or Thomism; yet they may also appear to be as critical of both positions as they are of pragmatism for overintellectualizing experiences that, in their view, cannot be grasped by the canons of formal or experimental logic. Theory and research in the behavioral sciences, such as psychoanalysis and anthropology, have also begun to influence work in educational philosophy more directly; usually, however, their effect is less to oppose Dewey's general approach than to supplement aspects of it that he developed insufficiently.

These and other streams of thought, which could be followed a long way, are mentioned for only two reasons. The first is to underscore the observation that educational philosophy today is in a state of extreme flux. We may take it for granted that all of its cross-currents are symptomatic of the fact that ours is a time of fumbling questioning and uneasy searching in every area.

The second reason brings us back directly to the theme of this concluding Part. It is at once apparent to students of religion that many of the same cross-currents are observable in this field. Linguistic analysis, existentialism, psychoanalytic and anthropological theory—these and other relatively recent but potent influences are being subjected to critical treatment by philosophers of religion just as they are by philosophers of education. Meanwhile, naturalistic humanism, as expressed by Dewey in *A Common Faith*, or by pragmatists such as Max Carl Otto in *Science and the Moral Life,* remains influential in the theory and practice of liberal religious institutions, while its educational corollaries remain influential in the theory and practice of American schools. Yet in both religion and education, advocates of more traditional orientations have recently succeeded in arousing public as well as scholarly favor to an extent that would have seemed unlikely even two or three decades ago. In both cases, moreover, I shall assume again that the reasons are at bottom similar—that they stem much more from an unstable milieu than from the intellectual restlessness of educators, religionists, or even of philosophers.

The religious and educational situation that I have tried to sketch in very broad strokes provides merely a backdrop. Negatively, rapprochement between the two great institutions is now demanded by virtue of the fact that, since both are caught in the same cultural maelstrom, both reflect in their philosophic struggles and gropings the same kinds of response to conflicting forces. Positively, the philosophy of education that should now emerge is one that attempts without compromise or regression to synthesize the richest new resources available to it. Among such resources are certainly those of religious experience and philosophy themselves.

I wish now to prepare the stage for elaborating my theme. Thus far I have avoided definitions of most terms, and so I have begged some questions. The three key terms, it need hardly be said, are *philosophy, education,* and *religion.* Justification for the projected synthesis depends, indeed, upon your willingness to consider (if not at once to accept) the definitions that I shall venture. All three definitions are governed by an assumption related to one already made in speaking of our time of trouble as the all-embracing context of our problem. Fruitful understanding of *any* major human problem requires that we study it in the cultural soil in which it grows and which, in turn, it nourishes.

Take *philosophy* first. In their preoccupation with technical questions, philosophers today sometimes forget what most of them would probably still admit if pressed—that philosophy is a creation of all cultures on record simply because all cultures have needed to attempt satisfactory interpretations of their own ways of life. The sophistication with which they have managed to express these meanings has varied tremendously. Yet anthropological research has found that even the most "primitive" cultures create systems of symbols—verbal, terpsichorean, pictorial, musical, and others—many of which succeed with remarkable delicacy, beauty, and profundity, to convey to their members the deepest values, the most honored orders, and the proudest proficiencies that they have been able to fashion in their evolutionary course.

Thus, while philosophy as a discipline has through many centuries proliferated into a series of highly skillful specializations, we should never lose sight of its original and most universal function as the supreme expression of cultural meaning. It is this function that is by far the most germane in considering philosophy's role in relation to education and religion. For both of these are indigenous manifestations of culture. Therefore, both must be included in any attempt to express a culture's meaning—that is, to philosophize about it.

Consider *education* in a similar light. Here the term "enculturation" is provocative. As used by anthropologists, it is defined as the inclusive process by which every member of every culture learns to live according to patterns of the culture. In universal scope, education, therefore, *is* enculturation. If it is distinguishable at all, education is narrower only in the respect that historically we associate it with formal institutions called schools, whereas the enculturative process is shared by all who condition, train, or otherwise influence anyone else, whether they be parents, medicine men, playmates, hunters, lovers, or kings.

We conclude, then, that just as philosophy enters into the full flow of human life when observed in cultural terms, so, too, does education. One characteristic of education as enculturation that anthropologists often underestimate, however, is that the process of learning to live in any culture by no means connotes merely fitting or transmitting. True, to enculturate a child necessarily means to teach him the customs, rules, and values of his own community. But (as is noted in Chapter 4) it is more than this, if only in the sense that learning to live in any culture requires skills of controlling the natural and social environment upon which the culture depends for its survival.

Enculturation, in short, involves learning to modify as well as to adjust, learning to revise as well as to accept. And while it is true that cultures differ widely in the extent and skill to which one or the other sort of learning is stressed, we detect in this aspect of enculturation the germ of education as a critical, active enterprise at the same time that it is a reinforcing one. We might even go so far as to declare that all cultures provide for innovation and novelty as well as for repetition and familiarity in their ways of life—a fact of prime importance in the building of any kind of educational philosophy that can effectively help to guide its culture.

And now *religion*. Like philosophy and education, religion is common to all cultures known to history, even though the ways in which it is institutionalized and celebrated vary at least as widely as do ways of enculturation. Amid these variations, however, certain common characteristics may be selected for their relevance.

One has been noted by the late eminent anthropologist, Alfred L. Kroeber, among others. Speaking of the major world religions—Christianity, Buddhism, and Mohammedanism—Kroeber finds that all of them were colossal forces in "the fundamental reorientation of civilization, in redirective change. . . ."[1] All three emerged, moreover, within the relatively short span of about a thousand years, all three in southwestern Asia. Thus, he contends that, regardless of their differences, all three religions were pointing the way through a common pattern induced by "the cultural set of the region and times."[2] Kroeber notes that these religions, like others, have also played a role of cultural conservation and fixation—a role that gains in influence as the original "redirective" influence declines. Nevertheless, it is significant that he highlights the former and not the latter cultural role of religious experience in trying to account for the processes of historical change.

Another revealing characteristic is suggested by the definition I submit in such a cultural perspective. *Religious experience is the search for, identification with, and commitment to the largest and most significant whole that man may envisage.* This definition, I believe, not only applies to every range of religious experience in cultural experience—theistic and nontheistic, supernatural and natural, pluralistic and monistic, complex and simple—but supports Kroeber's viewpoint that such an experience in its primary impact is one of cultural renewal. For the most vigorous periods of search for, identification with, and commitment to the most significant whole that man may envisage are motivated, I am sure he would contend, by the awareness of the sterility and disintegration of earlier identifications and commitments (in the case of Christianity, of course, primarily the Graeco-Roman civilization that it radically challenged and largely superseded).

Drawing together our abbreviated definitions of philosophy, education, and religion may help to focus the point of view from which we may now proceed. This viewpoint is an anthropologically oriented philosophy of education. Philosophy is now seen as both offspring and progenitor of cultural self-expression; education as the agency by which cultural patterns are transmitted and modified, one of its chief functions being to refine and promote such efforts as self-expression; religion as one of the major institutions through which both philosophy and education perform their respective roles. Thus, as a powerful galvanizer of purposeful cultural activity, religion becomes not only one of the most intriguing interests of philosophy itself but often a preoccupation of the enculturative process. By the same token, any culture that attempts, as ours has recently attempted, to segregate as far as possible all three cultural events from one another, and even to maintain that philosophy has little to do with either education or religion in their cultural roles (except perhaps to expose their "meaningless" language)—such a culture has drifted far indeed from the mainstream of the life of man.

I do not hold that the drifting has carried us so far that we no longer are able to push back to the mainstream. If we *are* able to do so, however, it is necessary first to recognize that the disturbances in educational philosophy and practice to which I have alluded are part and parcel of our time of trouble—more particularly, to observe that the shift in American education away from dominance of the pragmatic-experimental outlook toward various disparate alternatives itself reveals deep-seated cultural disturbances. Having made this appraisal, however sketchily, we must now turn to some of these alternatives and ask which, if any, may contribute to the beginning of a synthesis of philosophy, education, and religion when these are regarded as resources for cultural renascence.

11. Building Blocks for Cultural Renewal

If the philosophy of education is to shoulder the arduous task of rebuilding its own foundations so that our schools and colleges may in turn face their responsibilities with vigor and authority, the first and most difficult imperative is to come to terms with what we may call building blocks of cultural renewal. To be sure, many of these responsibilities are on the frontiers of research and theory. And all are fraught with questions and doubts awaiting further exploration.

The array of opportunities available to a philosophy of education appropriate to our age is so overwhelming, moreover, that no two builders would choose exactly the same ones. Certainly my own choices are debatable. Nevertheless, five such opportunities may be identified as indispensable. Their bearing upon the relation of education and religion will, I hope, become more and more apparent as we move toward the concluding chapter.

For want of more accurate terms, let me call these, first, cultural operationalism; second, epistemological sociologism; third, psychodynamism; fourth, existentialism; and fifth, evolutionism. Each of these terms points to further controversy. None, therefore, can be treated except in a suggestive way, and then only insofar as it bears directly upon the needed partnership.

Cultural operationalism connotes a fusion of several strains of ideas. The cultural component has been anticipated in preceding chapters, but in somewhat different contexts. Perhaps the single most fertile concept of the past seventy-five years of social science, "culture" has provided a new framework for interpreting human experience in terms of patterned relationships of spatial and temporal order. The core characteristic of these relationships is that they are not inherited genetically but are transmitted and modified by each succeeding generation through man's enculturative capacity to teach and to learn. It is a capacity remarkably manifested in symbolic forms, of which written and spoken language is at once the most highly complex and the most necessary to cultural dynamics.

By "operationalism" I mean the idea that men invent many of their symbols for the purpose of shaping their environment—that is to say, operating on it through explanation and control. The theory that these symbols are intellectual tools gradually hammered out of the need to achieve increasing mastery over physical, biological, and human nature anticipates, in turn, the concept of evolutionism. Operationalism in the philosophy of science was popularized by the physicist Percy W. Bridgman. But it was first developed systematically by Charles Peirce, and extended to the whole human enterprise by Dewey.

The idea of cultural operationalism has double significance for us. On the one hand, it epitomizes the central feature of culture as an acquired rather than inherited phenomenon of human nature. As Ernst Cassirer suggests in his characterization of man as *animal symbolicum,* culture on every level of complexity is carried on by symbolic means. To be sure, magical symbols are distinguished from scientific ones by the fact that the former acquire their own status as objects of reality, whereas scientific symbols (as well as those of art and philosophy) are recognized as human creations for accomplishing human purposes. Cassirer has made us aware—perhaps more clearly than any other philosopher—of the far-reaching importance of this distinction. Magical symbols, he insists, are not limited to primitive cultures; they remain powerful whenever men *reify* their symbols—that is, whenever the symbols of, say, church or state are treated as things possessing objectivity in and of themselves.

Following from the operational theory of symbolism, culture may itself be treated as an operational concept—a position that the anthropologist Clyde Kluckhohn supported with extraordinary acumen. This is to say that culture, too, is an "intellectual construct" invented to explain and develop certain levels of human behavior—notably, those above the merely biological and psychological levels. By no means all influential anthropologists accept this kind of operational interpretation (Leslie White, for example, does not); but then they, too, reify: they encourage us to believe that culture is a kind of self-contained, autonomous reality, subject to its own irrevocably established laws. From this nonoperational view, it is only a step to the assumption that all cultural institutions, from the economic to the religious, possess an equally superobjective status, even when room is allowed for them to evolve.

One of the values of cultural operationalism for educational philosophy is that it regards enculturation in the sense earlier noted—that is, as a controlling and directing as well as stabilizing agency. Moreover, it challenges the cultural assumptions of educational theories derived from such philosophies as Thomism and objective idealism, both of which objectify their concepts into eternal objects. Religious symbols for them are not, in ultimate meaning, operational; they are antecedently given realities which it is the first business of education to teach all cultural inductees to accept and to obey. The conflict between the educational philosophy of pragmatism-experimentalism and these historic philosophies may be viewed, in this context, as a conflict between cultural operationalism and non-operationalism. And because the latter is a much older, more habitual way of symbolizing, it is not difficult to understand why, during times of insecurity, its appeal increases in ways not wholly unlike the current appeal of authoritarian political movements at home and abroad.

The second building block, which I choose to call *epistemological sociologism,* is closely akin to cultural operationalism, but it throws light on the unfinished tasks of educational philosophy in ways that the first does not. Although it is similar to cultural operationalism in the respect that symbolism is again interpreted primarily in cultural terms, epistemological sociologism focuses more sharply on the role of symbols as instruments of one important feature of cultural patterns—that is, on their social structures and the systems of power that support them. The term "epistemological" is appropriate because it is, above all, the truth or falsity of social symbols that our second resource helps us to grasp more clearly than we otherwise could.

Two outstanding thinkers may occur to you as contributive to epistemological sociologism. (I choose "sociologism," which connotes the theory of society, rather than "sociology," which is now oftener regarded as a behavioral science.) One, of course, is Karl Marx, whose interpretation of class structure and class dynamics continues to exert literally explosive influence. The other is Karl Mannheim, whose Marx-influenced "sociology of knowledge" continues to deserve far more refinement and application than it receives.

The central contention of epistemological sociologism is that ideas are not only culturally shaped but are also accurate symbols of moral, political, educational, and religious experience according to how clearly and effectively they express the conflicting interests and loyalties inherent in class and power alliances. These interests and loyalties differ according to where or when they reflect the position of people of established status and dominance, and where or when they do not. The clear implication is that knowledge, or at least the kinds of knowledge concerned directly with human relationships, is far less "objective" and "self-evident" than conventional epistemologies have presupposed. On the contrary, such knowledge is so pervasively and subtly perspectival and situational that the only hope of achieving anything like "objectivity" about any instance is to accept the paradox that it is *not* objective, and then proceed to correct the distortions that only thus become discernible.

I question whether, without adroit utilization of this idea, it is any longer possible to construct an epistemology for education that can provide criteria by which to determine and teach reliable knowledge of man. Such an epistemology becomes, for example, a razor-sharp tool to expose distortions that commonly occur in social-studies courses purporting to teach American history or the nature of our enterprise system. Mannheim's theory that human truths (and, of course, values) are either "ideological" or "utopian" in tendency—that is, are either reconfirming or innovating in their response to any given political, social, and economic power structure—has sweeping implications for the kind of outlook conveyed to young American learners.

Equally, one may approach religious experience in ideological or utopian terms, or on a spectrum that includes both. Kroeber's contention that the great religions were in their early motivation chiefly utopian (in Mannheim's sense) illuminates their cultural significance as forces for cultural renovation as well as their later conserving, reinforcing, and therefore increasingly ideological role. Insofar as education includes religious influences within the study of history, it will ignore epistemological sociologism in its interpretation of them only at the cost of evasion.

Psychodynamism, our third building block, is the theory and science of selfhood. Whereas the first two building blocks are cultural and social, psychodynamism centers primarily in personality. The term further connotes interpretation of the psyche as fields of vital energies (reminiscent of Henri Bergson's *élan vital*) rather than as static structures of machine-like parts.

Although not without his own mechanistic biases, Freud comes to mind first when we think of the pioneers of psychodynamic theory, just as we are reminded of him in our model for experimentation in education for sexuality. The fact that his postulates and methodologies have been subjected to more than two generations of revision has not destroyed them; they have, if anything, been strengthened by more inclusive approaches. These do not repudiate Freudian hypotheses so much as they recognize that a mature theory of psychodynamism requires cultural and social polarities in a continuum with the polarities of individuality. As G. H. Mead demonstrated in another framework, the nature of the self is understandable only as a social self.

Still a different way to perceive the polarities of psyche and culture is to recall that both, in intriguing ways, correct the one-sidedness of philosophies derived too purely from the Enlightenment. Man is not the intellectual being portrayed by the rationalists and idealists of classical German and French philosophy. The emotional forces within him are cyclonic and often overpowering—a fact that Freud's theory of the unconscious established conclusively. Equally cyclonic, moreover, are the unrational forces manifested in cultural and social behavior—a fact that neo-Marxian theories of class conflict have likewise established. As various scholars have pointed out, Freud and Marx, in their common insistence upon the power of the unrational, are complementary, not antithetical.

And yet, as is also frequently noted, psychodynamism paradoxically may prove quite as rational in its effects upon behavior as epistemological sociologism is rational in its effects upon knowledge. Both theories assume that any hope for the flowering of civilization must derive from ruthless analysis of the unrational forces that permeate personal and cultural experience. The healthy personality requires an ego that has learned—often painfully and slowly, to be sure—both how to sublimate and how to discharge its libidinous energies, rather than merely how to suppress them. A healthy culture requires that its members have maximum opportunities to share and participate in its total resources without the coercions and "escapes from freedom" that autocratic power structures engender.

Interpreted as a complex of operational concepts, psychodynamism is indispensable to the kind of philosophy of education toward which we should now be aiming. The learner is always a self, so much so that in a crucial sense the single most valuable thing one can ever learn is the nature of one's self, including one's unconscious and preconscious nature. If such learning is to occur, however, the teacher must become aware of his own nature and of the invisible currents of cathectic energy that flow back and forth unceasingly between him and his learners.

The psychodynamic atmosphere of the classroom situation is often its most destructive or constructive feature— far more so than all the books and lectures and apparatus of the typical curriculum. As suggested in earlier pages, no teacher should be allowed to undertake his professional responsibilities until and unless he has been immersed in the theory and practice of psychodynamism, if only because emotional ill-health is as contagious as scarlet fever.

The choice of *existentialism* as our fourth building block is continuous with the preceding one, or rather with all three. Despite sharp differences, as are mentioned in Chapter 7, existentialism shares with cultural operationalism a mutual hostility toward the reifying propensities of traditional philosophies—propensities leading to elaborate schemes of reality that are impressive as speculative ventures but too frequently conceal the experiential processes, the nerve roots and the bloodstream, of nature and life. Despite sharp differences, too, with epistemological sociologism, existentialism equally condemns the hypocrisies and fabrications of theories of knowledge that claim to be rational but fail to take into account the existence of human energies that are anything but rational.

But it is with the third building block, psychodynamism, that existentialism reveals the closest kinship. Rollo May, an American exponent of the emerging school of psychodynamism called existential psychiatry, pays tribute to the father of existentialism, Soren Kierkegaard, as well as to Friedrich Nietzsche, Jean-Paul Sartre, and other contemporaries, and finds in Freud himself much that is existential in its implications.

Granting that existentialist philosophers are notorious

for disparities among themselves, their deepest mutual concern, as was noted earlier, is with man's intrinsic experience —his own ultimate and immediate existence that no amount of scientific analyzing or philosophic system-building can dispel or explain. To face oneself with utmost honesty is the most arduous of human tasks. But it is also tragic in that the very effort to do so exposes one's incapacity to grasp the total meaning of oneself, of other selves, and of the world.

Tillich, perhaps more searchingly than any American thinker, has sought to epitomize existential reality in terms of the anxiety syndrome. For him, anxiety is inescapable because no man can avoid the "latent awareness" that he is caught in the web of nonbeing as well as of being—that is, the awareness of his own mortality and therefore of the inevitability and mystery of the death that awaits him. But man is anxious also because he can never quite encompass the meaning of what Tillich called "ultimate concern." Or, to paraphrase the preceding chapter, one cannot, however desperately one yearns to do so, identify oneself completely with the largest and most significant whole that is longingly envisaged. More honestly, one can never envisage clearly and conclusively such a whole at all. The realization that ultimate concern thus forever remains elusive, combined with the realization that nonbeing must of necessity also elude one, produces in turn an inescapable sense of guilt and despair. The highest obligations of man to himself and to his world defy total fulfillment.

Yet, in common with other existentialists, Tillich challenges man to face his existence with courage, strength, and hope. "The courage to be" is, I think, the primary aim also of all types of psychotherapy—the courage to be true to one's own self in the face of the despair that lurks from birth to death in the caverns of one's nature. In Tillich's words, "He who is not capable of powerful self-affirmation in spite of the anxiety of nonbeing is forced into a weak, reduced self-affirmation"[1]—a condition that breeds not only neurotic and psychotic illness but the estrangements so habitual to our age of disintegrating standards and outmoded institutions.

Existentialism, thus, is an attitude as much as a philosophy. It finds expression, moreover, not only in religious but in political and aesthetic creativity. In art, for example, the existentialist mood is revealed whenever a novelist such as Joyce, a painter such as Pollock, a musician such as Cowell seeks to affirm himself with utmost integrity even at the cost of unspeakable travail. In this perspective, the subjectivism of so much art today may prove to be healthy, self-affirming protest against conventionality, artificiality, and imitativeness.

We have kept our fifth building block, *evolutionism*, until last because it proves to be a wonderfully integrative concept. No philosophy of the kind that should now be constructed can hope to serve education unless this concept occupies a paramount place in its over-all design.

Evolutionism is based upon an ontology of nature that embraces the astronomical as well as the geological, biological, and cultural. It views the entire universe, therefore, as an emergence of constantly new forms. In the words of Julian Huxley, perhaps the most influential living evolutionist, "All aspects of reality are subject to evolution, from atoms and stars to fish and flowers, from fish and flowers to human societies and values."[2] Evolution is defined "in the most general terms" as "a natural process of irreversible change, which generates novelty, variety, and increase of organization."[3] The epoch-making contribution of Darwin, who limited himself almost entirely to biological evolution, is thus vastly expanded.

Granted that the biological dimension of evolutionary

nature is shunned by disgracefully large numbers of public schools today, the prime significance of the broader concept lies in evolutionism as a philosophy of man-shaping-his-culture. The human level of nature differs from all lower levels in the respect that emergent change is no longer a product of the accidental concomitance of atomic energies and of genetic mutations leading to natural selection; rather, for the first time, it becomes a process subject to deliberate, planned regulation. Indeed, man alone, among all the animals on earth, may be defined as *evolution-directing*—a definition that opens thrilling possibilities for shaping the course of life, and, by the exercise of both creative imagination and concerned social action, for constructing a higher and nobler civilization than man has even approached.

Such global goal-seeking and goal-shaping is the primary intent of Huxley's evolutionary humanism. Not that he denies that man may refuse to take advantage of his powers to guide his own destiny, or that chance and blind struggle may continue to prevail in human affairs just as they do on the prehuman level. Still, he is not pessimistic. He could easily remind us that men have already learned *in some degree* how to plan their personal and communal lives—to conserve natural resources, to eliminate scourges, to improve the genetic structures of plants and animals by scientific breeding, to systematize economic and political events, even to release the gigantic forces of nuclear energy for humane as well as evil purposes.

Whether man will ever become the evolution-directing superhuman species of whom Nietzsche wrote becomes, in this context, the foremost question to be asked and answered by the philosophy of education. For when education is regarded as an enculturative process devoted not merely to transmission but, above all, to planned cultural renewal, then man's most necessary and most priceless invention becomes the refashioning of both the ends and the means of human evolution—an invention vastly more powerful and universal than that of merely formal techniques of teaching and learning, or even of subject matters such as science and art. Likewise, education becomes not so much a past-directed or even present-centered enterprise as it is the creator and shaper of audacious future purposes. Most crucially of all, education enables evolution to converge toward the unity of mankind as a whole, transcending national, class, racial, and other pluralities, while ever nourishing the novelty and variety that remain as necessary to the evolutionary process as unity itself.

To begin to integrate all five powerful building blocks of recent thought requires the construction of a philosophy of education permeated with religious quality. Although one can hardly hope to unify these resources sufficiently to eliminate all traces of eclecticism, one can observe how they supplement and reinforce one another.

I venture a term for this looming synthesis: *existential humanism.* Whether its meaning is expressed from the vantage point of education or of religion is less germane at the moment than to recognize that existential humanism represents a philosophy of modern man that is both educational and religious at the same time.

In their contributions to this kind of cultural self-expression, our five resources interpenetrate in innumerable ways. Cultural operationalism (the most distinctively American of them) is the copartner of evolutionism: man learns to direct culture as he tests out more and more experimental means of attacking the problems of human as well as physical and biological experience. As Dewey pointed out in his early essay on the philosophic influence of Darwin's discovery, evolution as a scientific concept destroyed the whole paraphernalia of permanent and preordained forms;

utopian role for our emerging age that Kroeber finds in the florescent periods of great religions of an earlier age. Radical contrast between the latter and existential humanism lies, not in departing from the delineating features of religious experience as a universal human want, but in wellsprings of thought and research, still largely untapped, that were not available to those traditional religions. Such wellsprings include the comparatively new sciences of self and culture. But they include also the existential attitude that undergirds and envelops them as sciences. Always, the religious quest of humanity is toward the ultimate concern which it is capable of envisaging. Magnetized and dramatized by the goals of the evolutionary humanist, education's first obligation is, in turn, to canalize and release its own vast capacities in behalf of that quest and that concern.

12. Philosophy of Education
as Philosophy of Religion

The cross-purposes and bewilderments that
now embroil American schools are, I have contended, the
consequence of a time of trouble that extends far beyond
immediate events. These cross-purposes and bewilderments
demand for their reinterpretation a philosophy of culture,
and therefore of education and religion—a philosophy at
once world-revolutionary and world-embracing.

The recent shift to a defensive position by the most
influential philosophy of education to have emerged in the
United States is the effect of an awareness, only partially
expressed, that pragmatism-progressivism does not satisfy
this demand as a philosophy of culture, as an educational
theory, or as a religious experience.

It does not satisfy the demand as a philosophy of culture
because its master concept, cultural operationalism, while
fruitful and necessary, fails to take adequate account of the

power of unrational social and psychical forces, or of the tragic insights revealed by the existentialist philosophy of human life and death.

It does not satisfy the demand as an educational theory because, while appreciation of evolutionary humanism is high, and while learning as experimental problem-solving is of prime importance to the function of education as enculturation, pragmatism-progressivism tends, by virtue of its very methodological fruitfulness, to place much heavier emphasis upon the dynamics of learning as intelligent practice than upon the goals and normative ends that such practice could and should serve—learning, moreover, that pays far closer attention to conscious dimensions of human experience than to unconscious dimensions.

Nor does pragmatism-progressivism satisfy the demand for religious experience. Despite Dewey's own penetrating intimations of what this experience could mean, his philosophy has not had its dominant impact on substantive commitment to or identification with the highest purposes of human existence. Rather, the major impact has been on processes of growth and evolutionary change, which usually turn out to be these highest purposes.

And yet, despite the recent aggressiveness of philosophies of education grounded in classical doctrines, such as Thomism and objective idealism; despite also the comfort that they take in the attacks upon Dewey by conservatives in education, any expectation they entertain that American education will return to their own orientation is, I think, merely wishful. These educational theories, although many of their advocates are astute, are much less equipped to cope with the conflicts of our age than is the theory they reject. For they derive their inspiration and their influence from the beliefs and practices of an age that has faded to a shadow of its original authority over much of the earth. It was an age which, in the young centuries of Christianity,

Mohammedanism, and Buddhism, did, to be sure, release vast human energies and did create institutions, forms of art, and philosophies of culture that were fructifying, novel, awesome, and often very beautiful. But it was an age that knew virtually nothing of operational thinking, that preceded evolutionism, that was unable to explain or control class power or class conflict, that possessed almost no scientific theory of psychodynamism. It was an age that erected much of its religious and political edifice on reified and even magical symbols, with their power to frighten and tyrannize. It was an age that denied participation by the great majority of human beings in the ordering of their communities or the planning of their futures.

Moreover, as theories of education, Thomistic and idealistic doctrines continue to assume that enculturation is more fundamentally a process of transmission than of innovation. Therefore, their theories of learning and teaching become largely ideological in their over-all effects—largely devoted, that is to say, to reinforcing rather than rehabilitating cultural goals, practices, and institutions. As religious outlooks, finally, they rest upon the premises of one or another form of traditional theism and transcendentalism—premises that again reflect a fading cultural epoch much more than they do the emergence of a humanity possessed with revolutionary knowledge, both of the world and of men's capacities to regulate and shape it.

I return, then, to the rejuvenation of a philosophy of education in partnership with the philosophy of religion. Utilizing the building blocks already assembled, I shall presuppose these resources without often referring to them by their cumbersome names.

By a philosophy of education as philosophy of religion I mean a philosophy of culture-building and evolution-directing, a philosophy that provides man with symbolic self-expression, that generates confidence in his power to control and renew his life, that impels him to search for, commit himself to, and identify with the most meaningful whole which he is capable of grasping. This is existential humanism.

The synthesis that is suggested by existential humanism may be approached in terms of three great obligations: the *obligation of commitment;* the *obligation of critical creativity;* and *the obligation of design.* Each, we shall see, is interfused with the other two.

The commitment that education now requires crystallizes in the goals of a convergent mankind, whose ultimate concern is expressed partially in cultural renewal that planned evolution now makes realizable; partially, also, in the courage to be human—fully human—despite the core of anxiety that is never purged by virtue of one's being.

Or, to recapitulate what I have urged at several earlier points in this book, the radical purpose of a world civilization, conceived in terms of transcultural democracy, is required negatively by the threat of nuclear annihilation. And it is required positively by the demands of an integrated technology, as well as morally and aesthetically by the comparatively new recognition that creative potentialities are universal to mankind rather than confined to any nation, ethnic group, or race.

But the most significant whole that one can envisage is infinitely greater even than the whole of mankind. The dawning age of space, the discovery by astronomers that ours is indeed a galactocentric universe, compels us to stretch our imaginations to embrace boundless spans of space and time, to reinvigorate our primitive sense of awe and mystery on a magnitude vibrant with wonder yet simultaneously with despair at its ultimate defiance of comprehensibility. If, however, education is to embrace this kind of human and cosmic commitment, we shall have to recognize the place that *myth,* properly defined, must occupy in education's attempts to symbolize its goals.

What, then, is myth? The danger of its misuse lies, of course, in the magical or reified role that it has played throughout cultural history. Yet, despite that danger, there is no reason (as Cassirer demonstrates) why mythical symbols need assume that kind of role—why, on the contrary, they cannot be recognized strictly as symbols rather than as overpowering, absolute objects.

Education for our age, at least as much in America as anywhere in the world, requires a "new mythology." The religious experience as it should be incorporated in learning and teaching will remain a merely intellectual object for scholarly disputation until it is clothed with the excitements of ritualistic celebration. But let us not forget Cassirer's warning that myths become ominous when, as in "the myth of the state," men begin to worship symbols as things of final, supremely coercive power. The obligation of education is to maintain the distinction at all times between symbol and reality, while yet providing, as powerful dramas on the stage provide, emotional immersion without the penalties of spurious identification.

One consequence, certainly, is that along with far richer study of the world's cultures than is now provided by elementary and secondary schools, the revitalized curriculum should provide opportunity to experience the aesthetic creations through which man has sought to express his most enduring values. Moreover, these values should be approached both through first-hand study of religious institutions and through the magnificence of religious arts. Anyone, for example, who has read Irving Stone's *The Agony and the Ecstasy* must appreciate how Michelangelo conveyed the spirit of his culture and religion still more influentially through sculpture, painting, and architecture than did any of the philosophers or church dignitaries of the Renaissance.

It is thus that the greater and more meaningful whole than oneself becomes both intellectually and emotionally impressed upon one. And it is also through the media of the arts that education may today contribute much to the planetary renascence demanded by our time.

Turning to the obligation of critical creativity, the pivotal point is that, if genuine education is to occur, commitment to and identification with the goals we have been envisaging must safeguard and enhance the integrity of self. Such integrity is epitomized by one's right to create uniquely, to think searchingly, to discover one's own distinctive capacities, and to act courageously in their behalf.

One fundamental difference from traditional philosophies of education and religion centers in this right. If commitment is not to be fanatic or dogmatic, it must be sought freely, openly, cooperatively. Here, particularly, the operational concept is so paramount that alternative philosophies of education must be accused of substituting their own pre-established dicta for experimental methods of inquiry.

But we may be accused here, too, of contradiction between whole-hearted commitment, on the one hand, and critical open-mindedness, on the other. I do not, however, accept the validity of such an accusation. The evolutionary goal of a convergent mankind is not a teleological end that we must accept because it is inherent in some kind of Aristotelian ontology. Nor is it a purpose in which we are forced by some fearsome power to believe on pain of punishment. Rather, it is a realizable objective for which human beings everywhere can choose to fight and work if they decide that it is worth all the planning, foresight, sacrifice, and powerful concerted action that is certainly required. In a scientific sense, it is, if you will, a hypothesis eminently worth testing. Yet, it is equally a myth in that it generates profound emotional identification among those who search for ways to express its meaning as ultimate concern.

Some persons and groups, to be sure, will probably never seek nor accept convergent mankind as their dominant objective. But these must never be punished for their dissenting roles. The operational way of attacking human problems is a completely public—indeed, the only democratic—way. Just as science progresses as much by its skepticism toward "established" law as by proof of its hypotheses, so too does education progress when concerned with intelligent learning—that is to say, with *experimental enculturation.*

As an illustration of critical creativity, let me define a concept and urge an experiment in religious education. The concept is "defensible partiality." By it, I mean that democratic learning consists of searching for answers to the most pressing human problems through comparative investigation of as many alternative approaches as are available—always with a view to arriving at the most plausible, in the sense of evidentially grounded and cooperatively attained, conclusions that such investigations can provide. The partialities that then emerge (they may not do so in some instances because the alternatives remain too conflictive) are regarded as defensible in that they have been constructed out of a dialectic of "due process" that has exposed them to their own vulnerable features, that has compelled them to modify and correct such features, and that compels them to be supported by the strongest, most reliable testimony and agreements that are available through evidence and communication.

Clearly, defensible partiality is a normative standard of learning seldom, if ever, fully achieved. Yet it remains a standard to be sought after and approximated. That it is not approximated oftener can be attributed to the fact that it is not even attempted by much of what proceeds by the name of public education. Continuous, widespread practice with it in the classrooms of America would contribute immensely to its effectiveness and fruitfulness. At the same time, the whole quality of democracy would itself heighten. For, in a certain sense, defensible partiality is the mind and heart of the democratic ethos epitomized in educational terms.

I include the metaphor "heart" because the principle is not to be viewed as a purely intellectual process. The deepest problems of human life are never merely intellectual. They are at least equally emotional. They are also ethical. Undoubtedly, one reason—not often enough expressed— why education has shied away from the religious phenomena of life is not so much that they are a taboo subject as that they appear too overwhelming to comprehend at all. But to concede this formidable obstacle is no reason to shun it; on the contrary, the very complexity of religious life is one good reason why it should *not* be avoided. Education is perhaps the one area in which approaches to the most urgent problems of human existence have a chance of controlled understanding and sustained resolution.

How, then, should the principle of defensible partiality function in the study of religion? Proceeding from the Supreme Court decision of 1963 that prohibits indoctrination but, by inference, encourages nonsectarian study, I suggest that we set up projects in a few carefully selected public schools, at first on the senior high-school level and then moving downward. As in the suggested project in sex education, teams of teachers, chosen for their interest, competence, and fair-mindedness, would receive preliminary in-service training of several months. As far as the religious composition of their communities permit, these teams should represent several religious orientations—theist and nontheist. Other major orientations, such as the Buddhist, will probably have to be represented vicariously through films and readings. The selected teachers frankly indicate to students their own religious preferences, at the same time agreeing to cooperative study in which such preferences are compared critically with others. Participating students likewise represent various orientations and likewise share these with their fellows. Resource persons professionally involved in religious activities are frequently brought into the project for lecture and discussion. Often, too, the student group visits religious institutions, observes ceremonials, and participates directly in them. Intensive study of the history, psychology, and philosophy of the religions directly represented by teachers and students is supplemented by similar study of religions not directly represented. Parents, who have been briefed on the project in advance, are invited to visit the project, to share their own experiences and attitudes, and to offer constructive suggestions.

As study proceeds, and as a mood of mutual respect becomes strengthened, students and teachers frequently take stock of their progress. By "progress," I mean development of the beginnings of consensual validation both as to any common qualities among the represented religious orientations as well as to their differences. I mean also indications of harmonious commitments that may emerge among the participants, or, what must equally be respected, indications of dissent from any such commitment. At no time is pressure exerted to force choices; teachers are ever alert to temptations to manipulate learners, either on their own part or on that of visiting resource persons. Continuous sensitivity to and exposure of propagandistic practices are essential. The outcome of the project is never predetermined, except in one respect—to achieve defensible partiality among as wide a proportion of the participants, teachers and students together, as the process permits.

Such a pilot project leaves open the contingency that learners will not reach the kind of commitment that I believe now to be imperative—indeed, it is certain that some will not. This is a chance we must take in democratic education. I also believe, however, that given the conditions required for defensible partiality to operate (it is itself, of course, an operational principle), the likelihood is great that many learners will move toward refashioning their own commitments in the direction of an existential humanism.

Confidence in this likelihood is strengthened when we return to two other aspects of the obligation of critical creativity. One is provided by the building block of psychodynamism; the other by existentialism. For please remember that this entire obligation centers in the integrity of selfhood. Psychodynamism is, I have no doubt, a priceless resource in developing such integrity. Everything that I have tried to say about selfhood focuses on maximum awareness, maximum channeling of emotional and intellectual energy in behalf of what Erich Fromm calls "man for himself"— "the fully productive character." This kind of person is not likely to settle for any form of education and religion that frustrates and blocks, that negates rather than affirms, that generates fear and insecurity, that substitutes reified symbolism—"the deification of things"—for operational intelligence and cultural renewal. Here is a major reason, too, why defensible partiality, when it is tested educationally in the laboratories of religious experience, will almost certainly result for many learners in compelling, passionate commitment to the evolutionary goals of man and nature rather than to the transcendental-theistic goals of those ideologically weighted philosophies of education and religion that still dominate so much of Western culture.

Another related aspect of the obligation of critical creativity is provided by the existential attitude. It is significant that Fromm is committed to the goals of evolutionary humanism while yet recognizing that the ultimate concerns of existence reach even beyond these goals. On the one hand, he writes that "man will attain the full capacity for objectivity and reason only when a society of man is established above all particular divisons of the human race, when loyalty to the human race and to its ideals is considered the prime loyalty that exists."[1] On the other hand, he also writes:

> One aspect of religious experience is the wondering, the marveling, the becoming aware of life and of one's own existence, and of the puzzling problem of one's relatedness to the world. Existence, one's own existence and that of one's fellow men, is not taken for granted but is felt as a problem, is not an answer but a question. . . . One who has never been bewildered, who has never looked upon life and his own existence as phenomena which require answers and yet, paradoxically, for which the only answers are new questions, can hardly understand what religious experience is.[2]

The existential attitude also enriches the obligation of critical creativity through aesthetic expression. Any kind of education that relegates the arts to a minor place in the curriculum, that treats painting, the dance, music, and other creative experiences as luxuries and frills, fails just as badly as the kind of education that disregards science. And yet, as most of us may recall from our own schooling, the teaching of arts that does occur is more often dull and imitative than it is productive of the unique expressive potentialities that so often exist in the preconscious recesses of young personalities. In this connection, the idea of myth is essential, especially as psychodynamic and existential resources are brought to focus on the aesthetics of religious experience, not only in past and present cultures, but, above all, in the achievable future of existential humanism.

The third great obligation I have called *design*. The philosophy of education should concern itself not only with the obligation of commitment (that is, to the religiously infused *ends* of cultural evolution); not only with the obligation of critical creativity (that is, to the operational, psychodynamic, and existential *means* by which a convergent mankind may eventuate); but also with the order of knowledge (that is, of experience that can provide substance to and fusion of ends and means).

What I am suggesting, in short, is a design for the curriculum of tomorrow's education that is at once scientific, aesthetic, and religious in all the senses of these terms implied hitherto. Such a design may be conceived as a series of widening concentric circles, the innermost core of which is the *intrapersonal* relations of the psychodynamic and existential self to itself. The middle circles radiate outward from the *interpersonal* relations of husband, wife, and children to racial, class, and other *intragroup* and *intergroup* relations. Finally, the outermost circles of the *intrareligious* and *interreligious*, the *intranational* and *international*, the *intracultural* and *intercultural* embrace the whole of humanity. Beyond even these circles, one may place those of the earth's relations to the solar system, of the Milky Way galaxy, and of the cosmos of infinite expanding energies and unanswered questions.

To complete the image, one should remember that streams of knowledge and experience weave in and out among all the circles from the innermost to the outermost —from the microcosmic self in the center to the macrocosmic whole at the periphery. When so conceived, this design provides a normative conception for education that applies just as properly to kindergarten as to college and adult education. To be sure, it is a radical design because it substitutes for the hodgepodge of disorganized, atomistic courses and skills that now typify the curriculum a single integrative principle. No matter what the particular subject (physics or mathematics, language or art, philosophy or psychology), every phase of learning is infused with the over-all theme of the struggles and goals of mankind itself.

Such a design, as suggested earlier, will require the elimination of certain conventional subjects. Certainly it will include many, such as psychiatry and anthropology, that are now almost entirely excluded from the public schools. A thorough overhauling is entirely proper, however—indeed, long overdue. Especially in our time of trouble, the cultural lags so chronic in education are indefensible. At the same time, the needed design will demand tough discipline and strong dedication from both learners and teachers.

The organizing principle of such a design is inherent in the five great resources of contemporary thought. But running through all of them is a single thread—the tragedies and anxieties, the loves and hopes, of mankind itself. When we now recall the term "an anthropological philosophy of education," this in essence is what I mean—a theory, a policy, and a program for schools at all levels and of all types, galvanized and unified by the nature of the human being as a personality, as a group-related self, as a citizen of the emerging world community, as an entity of the universe.

The education thus envisaged is by no means conventionally academic. Rather, it is aggressive and experimental. It encourages full-fledged participation in the affairs of culture. And it embodies the belief that truth and value are not the merely intellectual, bloodless entities that rationalism has so commonly taught but that they are at least equally the causes and effects of strong interests and allegiances.

This design for a mankind-oriented education is not, then, neutral or objective. It is governed throughout by the search for, commitment to, and identification with the strong interests and allegiances also inherent in the religious outlook, symbolized by existential humanism. In this respect, the design shares in the generation of a new religious-cultural dynamic comparable in power to that which, Kroeber said, was characteristic of the great renovative religious-cultural movements of past ages.

The philosophy of education thus conceived as the philosophy of religion is one in which the evolution-directing animal militantly exerts his scientific, aesthetic, and collective energies in behalf of one overarching purpose—the purpose of a converging humanity engaged in ever-restless, ever-anxious search for its own ultimate meaning and its own deepest fulfillment.

Appendix:
Reconstructionism

The term "reconstructionism" is commonly identified with a philosophy of education that regards the informal as well as the formal experience of learning and teaching as an inclusive process, one that both transmits culture and innovates culture toward the achievement of compelling life goals. The term is also associated with a strongly liberal wing of Judaism. Educationally, reconstructionism is much more a theory than a tested practice, although aspects have been applied, sometimes under that term, in many schools and colleges in the United States and elsewhere.

Reconstructionism is in the mainstream of naturalism. Therefore its ontology emerges from the empirical and realist traditions in the history of philosophy more than from the rationalistic and idealistic traditions. At the same time, it acknowledges and tries to incorporate in its outlook strains from virtually all of the important philosophic movements of the East and West—so much so that it undoubtedly reveals eclectic elements in its over-all formulation.

More specifically, the theory acknowledges the special influence of the pragmatic, experimentalist position in American philosophy; in fact, it is regarded by some interpreters as an extension of that position. In common with experimentalism, for example, reconstructionism regards experience as the key to reality, and it interprets mind as one important kind of experience—that is, as the functional capacity by means of which man is able to inquire into problems and act reflectively in solving them.

Education, for both the pragmatic-experimentalist and the reconstructionist philosophies of education, is the central instrument through which human beings organized in societies both perpetuate and continually modify nature, including human nature. But reconstructionists are strongly influenced by several strains of theory that are much less congenial to experimentalism and other contemporary theories of education.

One such strain is neo-Marxism. Reconstructionism rejects important aspects of the Marxian worldview, particularly what it regards as an outmoded ontology and epistemology, but it also insists that some aspects of Marxism have important lessons to teach both philosophy and education. Perhaps most fruitful is the theory of class power and class conflict. This theory, modified and updated by twentieth-century thinkers such as Herbert Marcuse, enables teachers, for example, to develop more sophisticated awareness of their own roles—to discover whether they are functioning chiefly as perpetuators of an economic-political power structure that proves in many ways to be undemocratic, and whether they should resolve the question of where their own allegiances belong if education is to serve as the ally of widening economic-political democracy.

Reconstructionists hold that teachers should "take sides" with "the forces of expansion" toward such a democracy, both in America and on a world scale. They oppose the Chinese and Soviet power blocs for their dictatorial systems, but they also oppose industrial-military monopoly and other types of economic minority control in the United States and elsewhere. They align themselves with the "radical democratic forces" that constitute a third, although as yet less organized and less powerful, economic-political movement, and they maintain that education's central energies should be channeled in support of this movement.

The contention that education neither is nor should be neutral in the wider cultural struggles of our time derives from a crucial assumption of reconstructionist theory— namely, that the period of history through which we are passing is characterized by unprecedented crisis. Traditional institutions and values are everywhere subject to severe strains. Some have already collapsed, and others have replaced them. The crisis extends, moreover, not only to political and social organization; it infects human personality, generates anxiety and other emotional ills, and produces in the young the widely recognized phenomena of alienation and anomie. Education therefore must assume responsibilities that might not be so pressing in a more stable period of human evolution.

For example, the contributions of Freud and his followers should be incorporated much more fully in the professional training of teachers, so that they may be better equipped to recognize and cope with the emotional disturbances of children who are, directly or indirectly, often the victims of the wider crisis in political and moral affairs as these impinge upon families and occupations.

Here the contention of reconstructionism that all levels of education should serve as agents of cultural innovation toward powerful and realizable human goals is paramount. Indeed, it is this contention that probably departs most sharply from progressivism and other prevailing views of education. From the psychiatric viewpoint, reconstructionism holds that mental health and personal happiness require an orientation toward constructive, realizable, magnetic life purposes. From the sociocultural viewpoint, the Marxian influence may once more be detected in the utopian goal of a "classless society"—a society redefined by reconstructionists in terms of "cultural designs" for planet-wide democracies in which major physical and spiritual resources are made available to and come under the control of the vast majority of the earth's peoples. Only such democracies, reconstructionism holds, can prevent man from destroying himself through nuclear war, pollution, overpopulation, or moral deterioration. Education is derelict, in turn, unless it uses its vast intellectual and aesthetic resources in behalf of the creation of a world civilization, directed by a democratic world government, and empowered to enforce its policies of peace and abundance.

This philosophy of education does not overlook the colossal obstacles that stand in the way of implementing its far-reaching proposals. It contends, however, that many of these owe more to inertia and misunderstanding than to deep-seated public opposition. Granted that some powerful groups oppose the reconstructionist policy or program because it threatens their own authority, reconstructionism also believes that large numbers of typical parents, teachers, and children in America and abroad would support it if given the opportunity. It suggests that beginnings can be made by means of "pilot projects"—experiments in curriculum, in teacher organization and training, in adult education, and in other ways.

One example is a possible design for the secondary curriculum. Assuming that, increasingly, young people will remain in school until twenty years of age, reconstructionism would test out a program of general education in which the entire course of study is integrated around one question: "What kind of world do we want, and how can we achieve it?" The focus thus becomes normative and goal-centered. Each of the four years would be devoted to one great area of reconstruction, such as economics-politics, human relations, the arts, and the natural sciences. Students would work constantly in teams as well as individually, learning all that they can about the present status of knowledge in these areas while bringing such knowledge to bear on the pressing questions of world conflict, survival, and renewal. Subject-matter courses in the conventional sense would be provided also, but even these would not be treated separate from the common theme. Thus a student could major in physics, say, but he would never graduate oblivious to the social or moral dimensions of his field. The same principle operates in the language arts, social studies, and vocational education. The aim would be to develop young citizens who are not only well informed about the most urgent problems of the twentieth century but also equipped with at least the groundwork of a worldwide purpose and a mature sense of responsibility to share concertedly with others moving toward such a purpose.

In a sense, then, reconstructionism is not merely a philosophy of education but a philosophy of life. Education is seen as the core of a much wider human sphere. For some of its exponents, reconstructionism is therefore a philosophy of religion as well as a philosophy of culture and of education. That is, it is infused with commitment to magnetic ideals, and it conceives of personality in terms of relations to a wider, more encompassing whole than the self—

an "ideal superego" that, while not defined in sectarian, supernatural, or transcendental terms, enables the human being to act cooperatively with others, and with emotional and intellectual dedication. The school, so conceived, thus becomes a religious institution.

NOTES

The author is indebted to the sources noted below for permission to publish the essays in this book. In all cases, the original versions have been revised.

Chapter One, "Agenda for an Ecumenical Congress in Education," presented at the Graduate School of Education, Harvard University, Institute for Administrators of Pupil Personnel Services, published by the *California Elementary Administrator* and reprinted in *The Education Digest.*

Chapter Two, "Imperatives for a Future-Centered Education," presented as the Boston University Lecture for 1968-69 and published by the Graduate School, Boston University, as "Our Climactic Decades: Mandate to Education."

1. E. A. Burtt, *In Search of Philosophic Understanding,* New York: New American Library, 1967, p. 198.
2. Robert Heilbroner, *The Future as History,* New York: Harper & Row, 1959, p. 186.
3. Kenneth Keniston, *The Uncommitted,* New York: Dell, 1960, p. 475.

Chapter Three, "Experimental Centers for the Creation of World Civilization," presented at the National Education Association, Sixteenth Annual Conference on Higher Education, published in the *Proceedings*, and reprinted in *The Journal of Human Relations*.

Chapter Four, "Illusions and Disillusions in Education," presented at the Fellowship of Religious Humanists, Third Annual Conference of Religious, Philosophic, and Ethical Nonconformists, and published in the *Kappan*.
1. As quoted in "Our Angry Teachers," *Look*, Sept. 3, 1968, p. 68.
2. *Ibid.*
3. Alain Touraine, "The New Industrial State on Trial," *Saturday Review*, Aug. 17, 1968, p. 56.

Chapter Five, "The Quality of Intellectual Discipline in America," presented at the American Academy of Political and Social Science annual meeting and published in the *Annals*.
1. Burtt, *op. cit.*, pp. 287, 291.

Chapter Six, "Confronting the Values of Youth," presented at the Connecticut Secondary School Youth Project Conference on Youth and published by the Project.

Chapter Seven, "Creative Ethics for Educational Leadership," presented at the College of Education, University of Rochester, Conference on Ethics and the Superintendency, and published by the University.
1. Michael Martin, "Understanding and Participant Observation in Cultural and Social Anthropology," in Robert S. Cohen and Marx W. Wartofsky, eds., *Boston Studies in the Philosophy of Science*, Vol. IV, Dordrecht, Holland: D. Reidel, 1969, p. 306.
2. In Israel Scheffler, *Philosophy and Education*, 2nd ed., Boston: Allyn & Bacon, 1966, pp. 225ff.
3. In Maxine Greene, ed., *Existential Encounters for Teachers*, New York: Random House, 1967, pp. 97f.
4. Warren W. Wagar, *The City of Man*, Baltimore: Penguin Books, 1967, p. 10.

Chapter Eight, "Anthropotherapy—Toward Theory and Practice," presented at a Supper Conference, Wenner-Gren Foundation for Anthropological Research, and published in *Human Organization*.
1. Marvin K. Opler, *Culture, Psychiatry and Human Values*, Springfield, Ill.: Charles C. Thomas, 1956.

2. George D. Spindler, ed., *Education and Culture*, New York: Holt, Rinehart & Winston, 1963.
3. Ernest Nagel, *The Structure of Science*, New York: Harcourt, Brace, 1961, pp. 485-95.
4. Milton Singer, in Bert Kaplan, ed., *Studying Personality Cross-Culturally*, Evanston, Ill.: Row, Peterson, 1961, pp. 65, 67f.
5. Erich Fromm, in D. T. Suzuki, Erich Fromm, and Richard D. Martino, *Zen Buddhism and Psychoanalysis*, New York: Grove Press, 1960, p. 112.
6. David Bidney, *Theoretical Anthropology*, New York: Columbia University Press, 1953, p. 51.
7. Fromm, *op. cit.*, p. 137.
8. Laura Thompson, *Toward a Science of Mankind*, New York: McGraw-Hill, 1961, p. 236.

Chapter Nine, "A Pilot Project for Sex Education," hitherto unpublished paper presented at the Advanced Doctoral Seminar, Boston University.

Chapter Ten, "The Restless Alliance," was presented, together with the following two lectures, at the Meadville Theological School, University of Chicago, and published in *The Journal of Human Relations*.

1. A. L. Kroeber, *Anthropology*, New York: Harcourt, Brace, 1948, p. 408.
2. *Ibid.*, p. 406.

Chapter Eleven, "Building Blocks for Cultural Renewal." See Chapter Ten, above.

1. Paul Tillich, *The Courage To Be*, New Haven: Yale University Press, 1952, p. 66.
2. Julian Huxley, in Sol Tax and Charles Callender, eds., *Evolution After Darwin*, Chicago: University of Chicago Press, Vol. 3, 1960, p. 249.
3. *Ibid.*, Vol. 1, p. 18.

Chapter Twelve, "Philosophy of Education as Philosophy of Religion." See Chapter Ten, above.

1. Erich Fromm, *Psychoanalysis and Religion*, New Haven: Yale University Press, 1950, p. 60.
2. *Ibid.*, p. 94.

Appendix, "Reconstructionism," adapted from *The Dictionary of Christian Education*.

Index

Aborigines, Australian, 62
Academic achievement standards, 73–83
Administrative group: and axiology, study of, 99–119 *passim;* and leadership, 117–18; role of, in sex-education pilot project, 141–42
Aggression, *see* Frustration-aggression complex
Allport, Gordon, 108, 114
AMA, *see* American Medical Association
America, status of, 72–73
American Anthropologist, 121
American Association for the Advancement of Science, 43
American Association of University Professors, student protest and, 39
American Federation of Teachers (AFT), 65; vs. National Education Association, 7–8
American Medical Association (AMA), 8; and Medicare, 10
Anthropology and linguistic analysis, 103–4

Anthropotherapy: defined, 130–31; and evolution, 135; and microcosmic studies, 135–36; participant observation in, 134–35; and psychotherapy, 131–34; theoretical prolegomenon of, 120–36
Arms race, 30, 31–32
Association for Supervision and Curriculum Development, 13–14
Atomic energy: and experimental world civilization centers, 45–46; future affected by, 42–43
Autobiography of Malcolm X, The, 67
Automated learning and teaching, 4, 75–76; and academic achievement standards, 75–76; vs. functional teaching, 6, 14; and means vs. ends, 17–18; self vs. society and, 14–15; worthiness of, 63–64
Axiology: diversity in, 134; for education colleges, 96–97; and educational administrators, 99–119 *passim;* resistance to, 122–23; *see also* Values

Becoming, 108

205